D1126106

CHRISTIANITY AND COMMUNISM

IS VOLUME

96

OF THE

Twentieth Century Encyclopedia of Catholicism

UNDER SECTION

IX

THE CHURCH AND THE MODERN WORLD

IT IS ALSO THE

40TH

VOLUME IN ORDER OF PUBLICATION

Edited by HENRI DANIEL-ROPS *of the Académie Française*

CHRISTIANITY
AND COMMUNISM

By *HENRI CHAMBRE, S.J.*

Translated from the French by R. F. TREVETT

HAWTHORN BOOKS · PUBLISHERS · *New York*

First Edition, April, 1960

NIHIL OBSTAT

Adrianus van Vliet, S.T.D.

   Censor Deputatus

IMPRIMATUR

E. Morrogh Bernard

   Vicarius Generalis

Westmonasterii, die XXIII FEBRUARII MCMLX

CONTENTS

INTRODUCTION

For several decades Christianity has found itself face to face
with Communism in many countries. Not to mention Russia
where a regime inspired directly by the Communism of Marx
and Lenin was set up as far back as 1917, Communist systems
of government were established during the thirties in Mexico,
at the end of the second World War in the Central European
countries—Poland, Hungary, Czecho-Slovakia and in part
of Germany (the German People's Republic)—as well as in
the Balkans, Rumania, Albania and Yugo-Slavia, in China
(1949) and Northern Vietnam (1954). In other European,
Asiatic and even African countries, there are more or less
organized, more or less influential Communist movements
which attempt to make inroads among the Catholic masses
in these countries. By its repeated efforts to overthrow the
regimes that have created the proletarian status, or more
simply in many cases, to transform or to secure the transformation of the living conditions of the labouring masses, by
its repeated appeals to a sense of justice and liberty, by the
constant assertion of its determination to free man altogether
from the fetters imposed on him in a world dominated by
private ownership of goods, Communism exercises a powerful attraction upon the working class in Europe and on the
more or less proletarianized masses of the under-developed
African and Asian countries. It offers itself as *the* answer to
the *real* needs of the masses imprisoned within the inhuman
structure of a world centred increasingly upon production. To
many it seems the only answer to the aspirations of millions
of men, since it points out to them the way to a tangible

future beyond the state of misery and hopelessness which is their daily lot, a future attractive to the masses in countries which, to judge from their institutions and their economic and social conduct, are too often only nominally Christian. These masses lost to Christianity in the nineteenth century, when European society was passing from the civilization of the *ancien régime* to that of industrial society, still have aspirations which in certain respects preserve their kinship with the Gospel. They are ready to listen to any appeal to a sense of justice and human brotherhood from whatever quarter it may come. The future which Communism offers them seems like the divine city of brotherhood evoked in the last chapter of the Apocalypse, only it can be made a reality here on earth. Under such conditions it is understandable that Communism can stimulate the energies and the devotion of good men.

If we add to these few brief remarks the fact that the development—amongst the rest—of the sciences of communication makes men increasingly aware that they hold within their grasp the means of unifying the world (this unification is in process of growth, it is true, as is most clearly shown by the conflicts that arise between great masses of men ill-prepared to meet one another because of the diversity of cultures, civilizations and ways of life) and that these means of unification are also means to power, we shall understand the truth of Fr Teilhard de Chardin's remark at Pekin in 1936: "An *élite* is tempted by Russian neo-Marxism not so much because of its humanitarian gospel as because of its vision of a totalitarian civilization closely linked to the cosmic powers of matter."[1]

Finally, we must also note that our epoch is characterized by the realization of man's economic and social situation, by

---

[1] Fr Teilhard de Chardin, *Sauvons l'humanité*, Pekin, 1936, reprinted in *Cahiers Pierre Teilhard de Chardin*: 1. "Construire la Terre", Ed. du Seuil, Paris, 1959, p. 18.

the introduction into human thought of the science of economics. But, at the same time, it seems that until very recently
economic science has developed under the form of a "physics"
for which man was an object—"the most valuable form of
capital"—rather than a subject. Hence a premium so to speak
has been unconsciously set upon the doctrine elaborated by
Karl Marx "within a total world of belief and thought", from
which man (or more precisely certain aspects of man) was not
excluded.

These few preliminary and introductory remarks are sufficient, we believe, to show that Christianity cannot ignore the
powerful human and, as it claims, progressive movement
which Communism is.

Yet at first sight it seems equally true that Communism and
Christianity should have no point of contact. They are on distinct and separate planes. One is a doctrine of spiritual salvation, offering to men of every age and under whatever political
and economic regime, the Gospel message of justice and love,
not in order to encourage a sordid exploitation of man's patience
and resignation in the face of the injustice of this world, but
in the interests of a real and spiritual communion in God.
The other takes its stand essentially and aggressively on the
plane of daily practical, economic, political and social
achievements. Yet to separate the two planes in this way in
order to make the distinction between them more clear is
fatal to the Christian faith, and is a refusal to see that at the
root of Communism—whether it realizes it or not—values
and a concept of man are involved. We must discover whether
or not these are compatible with Christianity. It is also a
refusal to see what Péguy has emphasized so well in one of
his reflections, "the spiritual constantly lies in the camp bed
of the temporal".[2]

Communism sets out to create a society and a "new man".

[2] C. Péguy, *L'Argent, Suite*, Œuvres en Prose, "La Pléiade", N.R.F.,
Paris, p. 1167.

For these, all reference to God will be abolished and man will be his own last end. These are the concepts at the basis of all the analyses and of all the economic and social developments which it proposes. Christianity therefore cannot fail to encounter and confront it.

Further, Christianity (Catholicism at least) insists that the Christian should not take refuge in an eschatological transcendentalism which would abandon this world to itself. The Christian must be aware of and fully accept the problems of daily life both for his own sake and that of his brethren. He must strive to find solutions into which the call of Christ's message will be well and truly written. The Christian's task is to consecrate this world to God. From the days of St Paul until our own, this task has always been a pressing necessity. Today, especially, the Christian must find within a total Christian experience the spiritual dynamism in economic realities. And this he must do better and on a vaster scale than in the past.

After so many books devoted to scrutinizing, to discussing and to bringing Marxist doctrine face to face with Christianity, why, it may be urged, are we to cover the same ground again? Why not be content to study how men, both Christian and Communist, actually behave? Why not point out all the implicitly Christian aspirations of the former, take due note of them and see how the implicit may be made explicit? Is not Marxism much more than a system that can be taken to pieces and put together again by more or less learned analyses? Is it not a hope, a life, and, in its own way, a faith for those who profess it? And we know that there is a considerable difference between the life the Communist leads and the ideas to which he appeals.

Correspondingly, why not point out what in the Christian's life is still not wholly Christian but an obstacle hindering him from spreading the light and the life of Christ among his brethren and more particularly among the working class, and this with a view to helping him in this latter task? Is not Christianity a life and is not this the essential fact?

We are well aware of all this aspect of the relationship between Communism and Christianity. But how can we be content with this point of view when we know the close link established by Karl Marx between thought and action in actual practice (*praxis*), when we know that the Marxist doctrine is the "guide for action" of those who direct the movement, even if, on the plane of daily life, other elements which existed before the advent of Marxism continue to influence the action of those who declare themselves Communists?

On the other hand the Christian's action must be as enlightened as possible if it is to be effective and at the same time free from all verbal and practical confusion. It is therefore advisable to analyse carefully the doctrine of action which Marx-Leninism is and to bring to light its fundamental motive forces, to show in what respect certain of its basic concepts are radically opposed to Christ's teaching, and finally to attempt to discover what demands are made upon the Christian by the mere existence of Communist doctrine. This is not to devote oneself to a Talmudic labour or to an abstract scholastic debate. It is to make clear the conditions of a deeper Christian presence in a world in full process of transformation, so that the emancipation of work may be a genuine return to human values and not the divorce of the latter from social life.

This task is all the more urgent since it has been possible to write, and with good reason, that Communism, "in its uncritical admiration for the tangible powers of the universe, has systematically refused to hope for its spiritual transformation. The human phenomenon, which is essentially defined by the development of thought, has thus been reduced to the progress of a soulless collectivity in the field of mechanical invention. Matter has obscured mind. A pseudo-determinism has killed love. An absence of personalism leading to a restricted or even a perverted future evolution and, by the same token, undermining the possibility and the idea of universalism—such, rather than any economic upheavals, are the dangers of Bolshevism."[3]

Fr Teilhard de Chardin, from whom we have just quoted the above reflections, continues:

> Face to face with a humanity which runs the risk of allowing the degree of consciousness already awakened in it by the evolution of life, to be absorbed into the "secondary matter" of philosophical determinism and social mechanisms, Christianity maintains the primacy of reflective, that is, personalized thought. And it does so in the most effective way of all, not only by defending speculatively in its doctrine the possibility of a consciousness which is both centralized and universal, but much more by transmitting and developing through its *mystique* the sense and, in a way, the direct intuition of this centre of total convergence.[4]

In this little book we are not trying to be original but to show by reference to previous works how Christianity is challenged by Communism. This we shall do by bringing together the conclusions reached in specialist studies and in those of men who have had to live in Communist territory and to bear witness there to Christ.

In the first chapter we shall see how during the last hundred years or so, the Christian attitude to Communism has developed and become clear in the documents of the Church's Magisterium, how the arguments formulated on the basis of the natural law and the Christian faith have penetrated ever closer to the heart of Marxist doctrine—its fundamental, radical and militant atheism. The second chapter will be devoted to an examination of the basic attitudes and the real intentions of Communism in regard to Christianity wherever they confront each other. We shall see that when Communism

[3] Teilhard de Chardin, *op. cit.*, p. 18.
[4] Teilhard de Chardin, *op. cit.*, p. 21.

takes issue with the Church apparently in the name of justice, or by criticizing her relations with previous regimes, it is attacking her as guardian of the Faith.

It will then be possible to relate this attitude to the main lines of Marx-Leninist doctrine which we shall discuss when we show that the points at issue between Christianity and Communism reveal two irreconcilable concepts of man. Then, in the last chapter, we shall outline some of those fundamental features of the Christian attitude which will undoubtedly help the man of today to rediscover the God of the Gospel.

CHAPTER I

THE CHURCH TAKES UP HER POSITION

For a little over a hundred years, the Church through her popes and bishops has put the faithful on their guard against Communism. It is important to know how this teaching has developed, for, in the words of Mgr Bruno de Solages:

> The Church's Magisterium is a living Magisterium. She is not content to repeat like a gramophone the teaching contained in her tradition in order to instil it into the new generations and to protect them against more or less heretical deviations. Aided by the Holy Spirit who, according to Christ's promise, is to "teach her all things", the Church from time to time brings forth from her treasury new statements—and thereby develops ancient truths—which, down the ages, meet the needs of individuals and societies.[1]

Within the terms of reference of Christ's revelation there is a development and clarification of doctrine. It is the Christian's personal duty to meditate upon this and to welcome it with loyalty and love.

There is obviously no point in looking for something new in every Encyclical or every word of the popes, especially in matters of dogma. But when we are dealing with moral questions new attitudes are less surprising, above all at times when

---

[1] Bruno de Solages, *Les Messages du Pape Pie XII et le développement de la doctrine catholique*, Chronique Sociale de France, janvier-février 1942, p. 11.

Christians are called upon to face major problems. This is the case for instance in regard to the problems raised by eugenics or psycho-analysis, in regard also to social questions. There is a more or less rapid evolution in the societies in which the Church is placed with the mission of "maintaining the deposit of faith", and in which also Christians are to labour so that normal living conditions are provided in order that men may be able to live in accordance with the spirit of the Gospel. The individual Christian and the Church as a whole are therefore naturally aware of new problems or of old ones arising with fresh urgency or in a new way. The Church, in the exercise of her magisterial function, naturally helps Christians to find their bearings and, as events occur and circumstances change, defines their obligations as Christians as these become increasingly clear.

This is the case in regard to Communism. Even a rapid and superficial glance is sufficient to show that this attitude is justified. The Socialism or the Communism of 1840–1860, of Charles Fourier, Cabet, Dezamy or Auguste Blanqui, is not the same as that of Karl Marx or Frederick Engels, which does not appear on the social and political scene until much later, although it was being worked out during this period. The Communist Manifesto, published in 1848, attracted very little attention at the time. In France it was not until the meeting between Jules Guesde and Karl Marx that a social movement inspired by Marxism emerged more than ten years after the Paris Commune. A fortiori, the Communism of Lenin, of Stalin and today of Mao-Tse-Tung, which inspires the leaders of the Soviet Union, of the European People's Democracies and of the People's China, as well as the European Communist parties, bears only a distant resemblance to the French socialist movements of the mid-nineteenth century.

The problems raised by the Communist League in 1847 or later by the different social-democrat and socialist parties, and those raised by the existence of the present Communist regimes in Europe and Asia, are not all on the same plane even if they have common roots and elements.

By a methodical analysis of the Church's teaching in the various documents of the Magisterium (principally the Encyclicals, pontifical allocutions, decrees of the Roman Congregations, bishops' pastoral letters), we shall become more clearly aware of the fundamental reasons for Christianity's opposition to Communist doctrines and to certain of their concrete applications.

Although the Church condemns Communism and certain forms of Socialism not for material reasons or on behalf of material interests but in the name of her religious mission to men (all of whom are called to live their vocation as sons of God), she does not think it beneath her to appeal in her successive declarations to arguments of a sociological character. Each document is therefore a complex assemblage of theological, philosophical and sociological themes closely interrelated. If we are to succeed in isolating these, we must distinguish them by analysis, but we shall not forget that we have to grasp them again in their unity especially when we have seen that one set of themes predominates over the others.

This method has the advantage of making it easier to understand the inner motive of the Church's approach as she tries to come to ever closer grips with the real nature of Communism, the advantage too of revealing more clearly the development of the thought of the Magisterium in this sphere.[2]

When we consider the documents of the Magisterium as a whole, we find that two series of arguments lie at the root of the Church's attitude towards Communism.

The first series is composed of arguments which, noting

---

[2] "If this doctrine (the social doctrine of the Church) is definitively and unequivocally fixed as regards its fundamental points, yet it is sufficiently broad to permit of adaptation and application to the changing vicissitudes of the times, provided that this is not to the detriment of its unchangeable and permanent principles." Pius XII, *Allocution to the members of Italian Catholic Action*, April 29th, 1945.

that Communism is opposed to the natural law and to natural rights, deal critically with some of the consequences of Communist doctrine and experiment. The second series (which is not entirely unconnected with the previous one) offers a closer analysis of the Communism directly derived from Marxism and is concerned with criticizing Communism's present forms.

A forward movement, a development from the implicit to the explicit, is easily discerned in both, while at the same time it is noteworthy that the problems Communism raises for the Catholic have changed with the development of the former as a more important fact in the world of today.

THE STARTING POINT

The *Syllabus* published by Pius IX on December 8th, 1864, includes Socialism and Communism in the same paragraph which condemns secret societies, biblical societies and the clerical-liberal societies which flourished in Italy and elsewhere during the years 1830–60. Recalling the previous documents of Pius IX's pontificate in which these societies had already been condemned, the *Syllabus* merely states: "4. Socialism, Communism, secret societies, biblical societies, clerical-liberal societies. Evils of this type are often the subject of condemnations couched in very strong terms in the Encyclical *Qui Pluribus* of November 9th, 1846, in the allocution *Quibus quantisque* of April 20th, 1849, in the allocution *Singulari quadam* of December 9th, 1854, and in the Encyclical *Quanto conficiamur moerore* of August 10th, 1863."

Examination of the Encyclical *Qui pluribus*, the allocution of Pius IX *Quibus quantisque* and the Encyclical *Notis et Nobiscum* (December 8th, 1849), shows that one of the arguments, repeated by Leo XIII in the Encyclical *Quod Apostolici* (December 21st, 1878), states that Socialism and Communism have as their aim "to destroy the worship of God" (*Notis et Nobiscum*), "to wage a fierce war against the

Catholic religion, the divine authority of the Church and her no less venerable laws" (*Qui pluribus*), leaving "nothing whole or intact of that which the divine laws have wisely decreed" (*Quod Apostolici*).

Pius IX protested, especially in 1849, against the revolutionary leaders who wished to proclaim a republic in Rome and in Italy, since schemes of this kind deliver the people over "to the criminal systems of the new Socialism and Communism" (*Notis et Nobiscum*, cf. *Quibus quantisque*). Fr Congar writes of the mid-nineteenth century:

"Revolution" means much more than the suppression of privileges, "republic" something much more and quite other than a political system, "the modern world" something much more and quite other than an aggregate of living conditions and a sensitive appreciation of certain values. Underlying these great categories which had become genuine "myths" was in fact a rejection of all submission to any authority higher than that of the individual conscience, a rejection implying that of the sovereign authority of God and in particular of God as revealing.[3]

COMMUNISM AGAINST THE SOCIAL ORDER

Pius IX protested against the attempts to set up a republic on the grounds that these were opening the way to Socialism and Communism, and that these two systems "are radically contrary to reason and the natural law" (*Quibus quantisque*), their doctrine is "destructive of the natural law" (*Qui pluribus*), and "it is not given to men to establish new societies and communities opposed to the *natural* conditions of human affairs" (*Notis et Nobiscum*).

We find the same argument in Pius XI's Encyclical *Divini Redemptoris* (March 3rd, 1937). Speaking of "Bolshevist and atheistic Communism", the Pope considers it to be a system "opposed both to reason and to divine revelation". Mgr Théas

[3] Y. Congar, "Mentalité de 'droite' et intégrisme", *La Vie Intellectuelle*, June 1950, p. 649.

takes up the argument again in his letter to the clergy and faithful of the diocese of Montauban in October 1944, "the Communist social programme is part of a doctrine of man, of society and of the world, contrary not only to revelation but also to the natural law". In his pastoral Instruction of February 22nd, 1947, Cardinal Cerejeira, Patriarch of Lisbon, says more explicitly: "Communism repudiates human nature. By its crass materialism it reduces man to the status of a mere piece of economic machinery. It rejects the certain facts of human history and divine revelation which prove to us the reality of spirit."

COMMUNISM UNDERMINES ALL AUTHORITY

Linked with these criticisms of Communism is another made by Pius IX. The Communist leaders, he wrote, inveigle the peoples into revolution "in order to attack the power of all higher authority" (*Notis et Nobiscum*), in particular the authority of the Church, of the family (*Quanta Cura*) and of governments (*Qui pluribus*). Leo XIII says more explicitly that they undermine authority by preaching "the perfect equality of all men as far as their rights and duties are concerned" (*Quod Apostolici*). It is the outcome of the ideas originating in the Reformation (Leo XIII Encyclical *Diuturnum illud*, June 21st, 1881). Pius XI wrote of Communism that it is "a doctrine subversive of the social order" and that it "rejects every hierarchy and authority established by God".

COMMUNISM DESTROYS PROPERTY

The attitude of Communism towards property is singled out for attack from the outset. Pius IX refers to it briefly in *Quid pluribus* (1846) and again in *Notis et Nobiscum* (1849). The Communist leaders provoke revolution "in order to pillage, ruin and invade first the property of the Church and then that of all other individuals" (*Notis et Nobiscum*).

Leo XIII returned to this question in 1878: "Misled by greed for the goods of this world which is the source of all evil, and the desire for which has caused many to err in the faith, they attack the right to property sanctioned by the natural law, and while they pretend to have at heart the needs of all men and claim to satisfy all their desires, they make a criminal attempt to seize all individual possessions whether acquired by legitimate inheritance, intellectual or manual work, or by economy, and to make them common property" (*Quod Apostolici*). He makes explicit the connection with the natural law mentioned in Pius IX's condemnation of Communism's attitude to property, and shows the disparity between the Church's position as it has been from the outset and the opinions based on the events of 1849. To substitute common for private property will do away with the stimulus of human activity and plunge the whole of society into want, as Leo XIII adds in *Rerum Novarum* (1891).

Forty years later, Pius XI cited as one of the aims of Communism "the complete disappearance of private property" (*Quadragesimo Anno*, § 120). In 1937, he said more explicitly: "Individuals are allowed no property rights over natural resources or the means of production, because these are the sources of other goods, and their possession would lead to the domination of one man over another. This is precisely why this sort of private property, as the prime cause of economic slavery, is to be radically destroyed" (*Divini Redemptoris*, § 10). In 1938, Cardinal Faulhaber refers again to this argument.

Pius XI's criticism of the Communist position takes account of the fact that we are now facing the Communism inspired by Marx and Lenin which draws a distinction between the ownership of producer goods and the ownership of consumer goods, while Pius IX's condemnations, and even to a certain extent those of Leo XIII, are directed against a form of Socialism and Communism inspired by Fourier, Cavet, etc., which

F. Ozanam described as follows in the *Ere Nouvelle* (1848):
"The modern school of socialists sees the root of all evil in
an iniquitous system of distribution. They believe they have
saved society by abolishing competition and by instituting a
prison organization of work which will guarantee to feed its
captives. This they have done by teaching the nations to barter
their liberty for the certainty that they will have bread and a
promise of pleasure to come."

COMMUNISM ATTACKS THE FAMILY

If, in Pius IX's view, Socialism and Communism destroy
human society because they attack religion directly, they also
do so because they subvert the institution of the family which
derives from the natural law. The Encyclical *Quanta Cura*
(December 8th, 1864), published at the same time as the
Syllabus, makes this clear when it notes that Socialism and
Communism seek to remove the child from a family upbring-
ing and from the influence of the Church.

For Leo XIII, the Socialist and Communist doctrines "dis-
honour the natural union of man and woman which was held
sacred even by the barbarians, and the bond of this union,
which more than all else keeps the home together, they
weaken or expose to the whims of debauchery".

In the Encyclical *Rerum Novarum*, after re-emphasizing the
nature of the relationships between the family and the State in
the sphere of private property, Leo XIII continues: "By
making the State the provider in place of the father, the socialists go counter to natural justice and break the links which
bind the family together."

In *Divini Redemptoris*, Pius XI states these objections more
explicitly. He examines the Communist concept of marriage
and the rôle which it assigns to woman in society when it
makes her the equal of man in every department of human

activity. The English Bishops have recently repeated this condemnation in their Declaration on Communism (Easter, 1948) as has also the Austrian Hierarchy in its pastoral letter (1950) on the Pontifical decree against Communism.

The Catholic Church is extremely sensitive in this matter since she holds the family to be one of the fundamental cells of society.

COMMUNISM AND LIBERTY

An argument mentioned by Leo XIII in *Rerum Novarum* when he wrote that Socialism leads to "an odious and unbearable state of servitude for every citizen" is repeated by Pius XI in *Divini Redemptoris*: "Communism strips man of his liberty . . . , it removes from the human person everything that gives him his dignity." This argument, which had not been previously developed, is also brought forward by the Canadian bishops of the civil province of Quebec in a collective pastoral letter of February 14th, 1950, on the working-class problem, as well as by the Austrian Hierarchy in the document already mentioned above. The French Cardinals repeat the argument in so many words in their collective letter on the decree of the Holy Office of July 1st, 1949, condemning Catholic membership of and collaboration with the Communist parties (Letter of September 8th, 1949):

> For more than fifty years the popes have not ceased to teach that under the prevailing labour conditions the position of the workers is an unjust one under both capitalist and Communist organization. The latter merely concentrates in the hands of an all-powerful State the privileges it takes over from private capitalism. Man cannot be an instrument of profit either in the service of private interests or in the service of the State. He must enjoy his personal liberty, he must see that his dignity as a worker is respected and he must receive his fair share of the prosperity which he helps to create.

Hence Communism is described as "Marxist totalitarianism" in contrast to "democracy" in the declaration of the National Catholic Welfare Conference (April 14th, 1945) which includes on its committee eighteen United States archbishops and bishops.

MORE RECENT REASONS FOR THE CONDEMNATION OF COMMUNISM

Socialism and Communism took on another aspect with the arrival of Marxism on the international political scene roughly at the time when the International Association of Workers was formed in London during the autumn of 1864, and when the social democrat or socialist parties were founded in Germany and France from 1870 to 1880. But it is not until the advent of Lenin and the Russian Soviet Revolution of 1917 that, in the documents of the Magisterium, specific positions are clearly adopted in obvious opposition to Marx-Leninism.

These positions, linked as they always are to revelation and to natural rights and a natural law considered as immutable, are the result of a closer examination of contemporary Communist doctrine recognized as a plan of action. The principal points singled out for condemnation are:

1. Materialism.
2. The class struggle erected into a principle of social evolution.
3. Atheism.

As we have seen, the arguments worked out in the past continue to be taken into consideration but yet give place to, or are incorporated into, a wider total view.

Materialism

The statement that materialism is a reason for Christianity's opposition to Communism was already implicit at least in previous documents, but in the thirties the Church went into the question more closely.

Although there is still occasional mention of "crass materialism" as a description of Communist doctrine, although there is sometimes observed in it "a philosophy of life based on the grossest materialism", both of which suggest that Communist materialism is founded on the philosophical concepts of scientific or mechanist materialism, yet it is in the Encyclical *Divini Redemptoris* (1937) that Pius XI points out the principal characteristics of historical and dialectical materialism. He does not, it is true, examine the meaning of this dialectical and historical materialism in the thought of Marx and Lenin themselves, he confines his study of it to the popular form in which it appears in booklets composed of extracts from the writings of Lenin and Stalin:

> The doctrine of modern Communism, though sometimes presented in specious and attractive guise, is really based upon Marx's theory of dialectical and historical materialism, of which the Bolshevist intellectuals claim alone to possess the genuine interpretation. The theory teaches that matter, with its blind and hidden forces, is the only reality which exists, and that it is matter which by a natural process evolves into a tree, an animal, or a man. Even human society is only a particular manifestation or form of matter, evolving in the same way and tending by an irresistible necessity and by a perpetual conflict of forces to the attainment of its final goal, which is a classless society. Such a doctrine obviously leaves no room for the idea of an eternal God, for a distinction between spirit and matter or between body and soul, for the survival of the soul after death, or for any hope of a future life.

> Developing the "dialectical" side of their materialism, the Communists maintain that the pace of the aforesaid conflict, which is to bring all things to their final consummation, can be accelerated by the action of man. They therefore make it their aim to accentuate the differences between class and class in the community; to represent class warfare, actually the source of so much strife and bloodshed, as a crusade of human progress; and therefore to crush utterly any opposition raised

to their systematic violence as though it were a crime against the human race. (*Divini Redemptoris*, § 9.)

At the time of the Liberation in October 1944, Mgr Théas noted that these rules of action continued to direct the efforts of French Communists. "It is admitted," he wrote, after acknowledging the answer given him by the regional office of the Young Communists at Montauban, "that Communism in 1944, as in 1937, is based on atheistic and materialist Marxism."

The decree of the Holy Office of July 1st, 1949, published on July 13th of the same year, which recalls the provisions of the Church regarding Communists and those who collaborate with them, itself also states: "Communism is materialistic and anti-Christian." The letter of the French Cardinals (September 8th, 1949), that of the Belgian Hierarchy (November 4th, 1949), and that of the Austrian Bishops (January 17th, 1950) also insist on this aspect of Communism.

The class war

In 1931 Pius XI explicitly stated that one of the aims of Communism is "a relentless class war". The latter is the motive force of social evolution, added in 1938 Mgr Gauthier, coadjutor Archbishop of Montreal, after the appearance of *Divini Redemptoris* (1937). It leads to the establishment of a dictatorship of the proletariat, noted the bishops of England and Wales in their collective pastoral letter (November 29th, 1936). As *Divini Redemptoris* pointed out, it is a passing but oppressive phase and the archbishops and bishops of the province of Quebec protested against it in the document quoted above.

From the moral standpoint its results are formidable for it leads to the establishment of a class morality. Hence Communism is a direct threat to Christian civilization, as the Belgian and Austrian bishops, among others, remind us in their letters concerning the decree of the Holy Office.

The fundamental atheism of Communism

Although in 1931 *Quadragesimo Anno* still pointed out, as did previous documents, that Communism is "the adversary and the declared enemy of holy Church and of God himself" (§ 120), although the English and Welsh bishops in 1936 emphasized that "the abolition of religion is a fundamental principle of Communism" (cf. the collective pastoral letter of November 29th, 1936), yet the Encyclical *Divini Redemptoris*, a year later, denounces in the Communist movement "a false idea of redemption", a "counterfeit mysticism" based on "a pseudo-ideal of justice, equality and brotherhood among workers". It sees in it something essentially anti-religious: "The theory of Communism is intrinsically hostile to religion in any form whatsoever."

Pius XII, in his 1942 Christmas Message, denounces Communism because it endangers the eternal salvation of mankind. Already in 1937 *Divini Redemptoris* had condemned it in several passages as atheistic. This is Communism's most serious defect and leads it to seek to replace Christian values by others based on an atheistic conception of the world. Pius XI made the purpose of *Divini Redemptoris* clear when he wrote: "Once again, therefore, we propose to summarize and explain the theory and principles of Communism, especially as they appear in the Bolshevist system." In 1944, Mgr Théas, in the letter already quoted, referred again to the atheistic foundation of present-day Communism. In December 1947, Mgr de Provenchères pointed out the different aspects of Communism and noted that it is based on "an atheistic and materialist" doctrine. The Portuguese Hierarchy in 1949 described the characteristic features of this theoretical, practical and militant atheism. After showing how Marxist atheism is linked with the humanist atheism of Feuerbach, the Portuguese bishops continue: "Communism might very well seem to be a purely economic and social scheme for the reorganization of society. But Communism as it exists, Communism in its present-day actuality, is essentially anti-Christian."

The decree of the Holy Office (July 1st, 1949) also insists on this fundamental aspect of Communism. Commenting upon it in their collective letter of September 8th, 1949, the French Cardinals connect the economic and social applications of Communism with this atheism: "The atheism at the root of Communism and present like an active leaven in all its economic and social applications, leads logically to the degradation of man. In the final analysis, atheistic Communism can offer humanity no other ideal than that of an ant-heap in which the individual is predetermined to a task whose purpose, method and ends he cannot understand."

In his radio message of September 4th, 1949, to the Bochum Katholikentag, Pius XII again made it clear why the decree of the Holy Office of July of that same year was promulgated.

"When a line of demarcation which no Catholic may cross was recently drawn between the Christian faith and atheistic Communism", he declared, "it was done with the sole purpose of raising a barrier against Marxist atheism and so of rescuing not only the working class but the whole of society."

The Church draws attention in this way to atheistic Marxism because she considers that Christianity and Communism are opposed to one another not merely on the grounds that Marxism criticizes the religious exploitation of man, which it considers to be one of the elements in the contemporary pattern of human behaviour, nor because it intends to proceed to a radical, practical and definitive suppression of all religion whatsoever. It is in the whole context of the Christian life that the Church meets Marxism as an opponent of truth. "It is the whole content of Christian dogma that is in detailed opposition to the content of Marxism."

Pius XII himself states this in the same speech to the Katholikentag when, after the lines quoted above, he immediately continues: "This decision has nothing to do with the opposition between rich and poor, capitalism and the proletariat, the haves and the have-nots. What was at stake was the preservation of the Christian faith, its maintenance in all its purity, the defence of the freedom of religion, and by the same token, the security of the workers' happiness, dignity, rights and liberty."

PRACTICAL ATTITUDES

Yet the Church has not been content merely to condemn atheistic Communism. Following St Paul, St Augustine and Pascal, she holds that in the concrete a man's behaviour is bound up with his religious convictions and that the way he acts influences the way he thinks and lives. That is why she feels under a strict obligation to draw the attention of her sons to certain lines of conduct as soon as these appear to lead to an implicit dechristianization of those who adopt them.

In addition to taking up her position in regard to Communist doctrine, the Church over the past few decades has had to interest herself in a new problem which did not arise before the first World War, namely that of day-to-day relationships between Catholics and Communists in the field of social, economic and even political life. Once it had become one of the important forces in the evolution of the modern world, Communism took up a new attitude towards Catholics with the advent in France in 1936 of the Popular Front. The policy of the "outstretched hand" towards Catholics was inaugurated by Maurice Thorez. The problem was not confined to France. It arose during the Nazi occupation of Europe for Catholics in various countries (especially Poland, Italy, etc.) with the setting up of National Fronts. Since the end of the second World War, the problem has become increasingly acute and urgent.

In passing, we may note that in the countries of Western Europe where the political systems are still liberal or pluralist,

it does not present itself in the same terms as in the people's democracies where the political system is that of a mass democracy.

Since the publication of Cardinal Suhard's statement to the press (January 31st, 1949) in which the problem is faced, an important document dealing with the question, the decree of the Holy Office already mentioned, has appeared.

The Church's attitude in this concrete sphere of the day-to-day relationships between Catholics and Communists is governed by the principles determining her position in regard to Communist doctrine. It is because of the atheism of Communism, which in her view cannot be separated from the political, economic and social action of the Communist parties, that "the Church cannot accept habitual and close collaboration" with it. At the same time, she recognizes that "circumstances may arise which involve Catholics in a course of action parallel to that of the Communists, when in the general interest there are definite, limited aims to be pursued having nothing to do with the objectives of the Party as such" (Cardinal Suhard's statement of January 31st, 1949).

The decree of the Holy Office gives more precise details of such cases but in the light of the same statement of principle: "Communism is materialist and anti-Christian."

The decree of the Holy Office reaffirms that the faithful are not allowed "to publish, distribute or read books, reviews, papers or leaflets which uphold the doctrine or the activities of the Communists", nor "to enrol as members of a Communist party or to encourage it any way", nor are they to profess "the materialist and anti-Christian doctrine of the Communists". In their commentaries, the bishops in the different countries of the world have laid down for the faithful of their respective dioceses rules for the application of the decree.

These documents of the Magisterium are an expression of its practical wisdom. The Church will not see her children

take the road to martyrdom without giving them warning, nor
can she let them run the risk of losing their faith. And, as
Mgr Ancel reminds us (in an article in *La Semaine religieuse
du diocèse de Lyon*, April 24th, 1950), this danger does exist
for a man who habitually collaborates with Communism.
Further, "he becomes responsible for loss of faith among
those who may be influenced by the Communist party with
which he cooperates". These then are the motives that guide
the Church's action in the practical directives which she gives
to the faithful.

LINES OF DEVELOPMENT

The examination of the different documents we have quoted,
incomplete though it obviously is, does reveal a certain number of significant features in the development of the Church's
thought.

The initial condemnations are vigorous, while those which
have followed later are more precise. Taken as a whole, all of
them, the older and the more recent, involve an implicit or
explicit reference to natural rights, to a natural law, neither
of which can be written off. This reference is hard for a Communist or a mind imbued with Marxism to understand, for
whom there is no *philosophia perennis*. "The philosophers
have only *interpreted* the world in different ways, but it must
be *transformed*" (Karl Marx, eleventh thesis on Feuerbach).
And so the documents of the Magisterium are not addressed
directly to Communists or Marxists but in the first place to
Catholics in order to remind them of the fundamental points
of Christian doctrine in relation to certain events having a
bearing on their own conduct.

There is a permanent element in all the documents which
we are considering—the reference to the natural law. But the
points at which Catholicism and Communism are shown to
be at variance are not always the same. The consequences of
Communist doctrine and action, which are called into ques-

tion in the more recent documents, are on the philosophical or strictly religious plane rather than the sociological. The opposition of Communism to the Christian family is always stressed. The problem of the different systems of private property is introduced more cautiously, although the right to property is always clearly asserted. In the concrete, indeed, the defects of the capitalist system have become more obvious than they were a century ago, when this system was in full process of expansion. In 1850 there was no question of criticizing the developing capitalist social system. Society stood on the boundary between two worlds, different in structure. One was essentially agrarian, the other industrial. This is no longer the case in 1960. We are immersed in an industrial civilization which, through its highly developed techniques of communication, brings together human groups whose cultures are divided by centuries of history. And in the process, it raises new problems.

Most of the recent documents of the Magisterium take full account of this situation. When (or sometimes before) taking up a position against Communism, the Church issues a criticism or a severe condemnation of capitalism. In *Quadragesimo Anno*, while recognizing that the capitalist system is not evil in itself ("it is not vicious of its very nature"), Pius XI denounces the abuses of the present economic dictatorship and its consequences and vigorously opposes the capitalism of the Manchester school. In his Christmas Messages, especially in that of 1942, Pius XII, whilst justifying private property, considered that "the positive juridical norms which regulate private property may change and more or less restrict its free use". The bishops of England and Wales in 1936, Cardinal Suhard in his statement to the press (January 31st, 1949), the Canadian hierarchy in 1950, denounce the abuses of capitalism or its dictatorship.

A no less important feature to be noted is the more explicit affirmation of the Church's opposition to Communism on strictly *religious* grounds. The principal complaint now brought against Communism, and from which the others derive, is that it is an atheistic and materialist doctrine. There are undoubtedly several reasons for this change of emphasis in the criticism of Communism.

This is due to the fact that the Church has understood more clearly that present-day Communism is rooted in the thought of Karl Marx, which is radically atheistic and has become better known through more recent studies.

The realization that Marxism is opposed to the truth of Christianity in every detail of the Christian life, and that the whole body of Christian dogma is in detailed opposition to that of Marxism, is undoubtedly of fundamental importance.

That the problem of the relationships between Catholicism and Communism is stated in this way is undoubtedly due also to the fact that the frontiers of religion and economics or politics have been better drawn and their mutual relationships better defined. The attempts of Christian philosophers and theologians to clarify these relationships have their repercussions in this field.

It is certain that all has not yet been said in the course of the development of the Church's attitude towards Communism. There are many outstanding problems both on the practical and the theoretical levels.

Frédéric Ozanam's remarks in his study of the *Origins of Socialism* are as relevant as ever they were: "When a question, for which theology, philosophy and jurisprudence always have an answer ready, returns at the onset of every revolution to terrify weak minds and to attract the strong, it may not be lightly brushed aside, nor are we to believe we have done with it by incarcerating a few hotheads. We must treat it with the respect due to the great problems which Providence uses to keep societies on the alert and to drive them forward along that path of progress where it allows them no rest."

CHAPTER II

COMMUNISM AND CHRISTIANITY

The events that have taken place in Europe, China and elsewhere over a period of almost forty years, while Christianity, especially Catholic and Orthodox, has been at grips with Communism, have been partly responsible for the Catholic Church's new awareness and attitude, to which we have referred in the previous chapter.

Before we investigate the nature of Communism itself, it is as well to see how it has behaved towards Christianity whenever, in the course of its development, it has encountered it as a living force. We shall examine this behaviour at two stages.

Firstly, after a brief indication of the way Communism acts in countries where it is not in political control (for example, France or Italy where there are important Communist minorities), we shall then see it at grips with Christianity in the People's Democracies of Europe or Asia, where a Communist regime has been established for almost fifteen years.

We shall then pass on to the case of the Soviet Union, where such a regime has now more than forty years of existence behind it. This will allow us to indicate more clearly the direction in which the attitude of Communism towards any form of the Christian religion evolves, once its power is solidly established.

In the pages that follow we shall not be writing a factual history. We shall rely on collected and published data and refer to books dealing with each country, and so attempt to descry the main lines of Communist method in its dealings with Christianity. This done, our analysis will allow a more precise description of the Christian attitude towards the present-day Communist movement.

THE PEOPLE'S DEMOCRACIES

While Communism appears as an essential force in the life of such countries as Poland, Hungary, Rumania, Czecho-Slovakia and East Germany only after the victory of the Soviet armies in 1945 and following on the creation in these countries of what was called "the People's Democracy", it had quite a considerable influence in the Western nations before the second World War, especially from 1936 onwards.

In the countries of Eastern Europe, its attitude and its activities in regard to Christianity are not the same as in those of the West, although the objective in view is identical—to divorce the Christian masses from Christianity considered as an obstacle to the advent of a Communist regime.

Therefore, before we consider how it operates in countries where it is the dominating factor in political, economic and social life, it is as well to recall very briefly its technique of action in countries such as France and Italy, where it is not free to do as it likes but has the benefit of the advantages afforded by a liberal democracy.

Communism has taken advantage of an economic or social situation far from favourable to the more or less proletarian-ized masses in countries like France and Italy, in order to appeal to all men of good will to cooperate in a progressive transformation of the status quo. At the same time it appears to leave to one side its own proper aims.

Hence Maurice Thorez, on the eve of the French parliamentary elections of 1936, made a resounding appeal on the radio. After painting a somewhat gloomy picture of the situation in France on the economic, political and cultural planes, he declared, carefully emphasizing his words: "We who have no religious allegiance, stretch out our hand to you, Catholic worker, wage-earner, artisan, peasant, because you are weighed down by the same cares as we are."

At the next congress of the French Communist Party, he spoke in greater detail:

> Our aim is not some sort of lowdown collusion with the Church authorities. Our aim is the union of the masses of the people in the struggle for improved conditions, liberty and peace. . . . We shall win over to the Popular Front and to Communism those who are kept far from us by their prejudices, in so far as we show them that Communism, our noble ideal, inspires devotion and service, in so far too as we show them that nowhere else will such a source of pure and generous sentiments be found.[1]

The objectives in view are clear, as is also the explanation of the method employed. There is no question of collusion between Communism and Christianity nor of abandoning any point of Marx-Leninist doctrine in any field whatsoever.

In his analysis of the appeal for collaboration between Catholics and Communists, M. Thorez did not minimize the doctrinal differences that separate Christians and Communists. "On the doctrinal plane, this proposal", he said, "asserts two things: 1. Communists are materialists and have no religious allegiance. 2. There is a *de facto* material, economic and social solidarity between Catholic and Communist workers." He went on to develop at length the Communist's materialist profession of faith. Then, on the authority of Leo XIII's analyses in *Rerum Novarum* and those of Pius XI in *Quadragesimo Anno*, he endeavoured to prove that the Christian and the Communist analysis of the real nature of

[1] M. Thorez, *La Mission de la France dans le Monde*, published by Soc. Intern. Paris, 1938, p. 120.

capitalist society had many points in common, and that this should lead to a genuine and effective collaboration in the practical task of urging concrete claims, in spite of doctrinal divergences.[2]

M. Thorez forgot to mention two points which are doubtless self-evident to a Communist listener, but which it would have been advisable for a Catholic listener to bear in mind.

1. That the Communist's view of *praxis*, i.e. the relationship of thought to action, makes him consider it inevitable and necessary that action should determine men's thought and their ideas. Action inspired by Marxism is therefore bound to lead to the adoption of the Marxist view of reality. 2. That propaganda will continue its efforts in every direction.

This policy of the "outstretched hand" to Catholics was revived immediately after the second World War. As it developed, it was accompanied by a denunciation—very virulent at times—of what the Communist organs call the "upper clergy". Under the fallacious pretext of an alleged collusion between American imperialism, the Fascist parties and the Vatican, the latter was the object of numerous criticisms. This denunciation of the Catholic hierarchy was kept up more or less vigorously during the years that followed. For instance, a resolution of the French Communist Party's Central Committee called for "resistance to the reactionary opposition of the cardinals and princes of the Church to the union of Communists and Catholics". This was a counter-move against the "decree of the Holy Office concerning Communism" of the previous July.

In order to win over wavering Catholics, a subtle distinction was made between *assimilation* and *acceptance* of the Communist programme: "The formula that lays down the conditions of membership of the Party does not mention

[2] M. Thorez, *Pour l'union, Communistes et Catholiques*, Soc. Intern, Paris, pp. 14–31.

assimilation but only acceptance of its programme."[3] After criticizing the declarations of the pope and those of the French bishops in favour of peace, as designed to sow discord, the argument continues: "Against this sort of manœuvre, Communists should do everything to consolidate and extend common action with Catholics. We shall be working for the consolidation and extension of this unity if we explain to Catholics—without attacking their faith—the reactionary character of the policy of the Vatican and of the ecclesiastical hierarchy, if we also help them to see the true meaning of these ideological campaigns which in fact have nothing to do with the defence of religion."[4]

The policy of the "outstretched hand" to Catholics with its corollary—a cleavage between the faithful and the hierarchy—ultimately implies the claim that in practice the Communist Party should be the arbiter and the guardian of Christian faith and Christian attitudes of mind for those Christians who accept such a situation.

The Church has reacted vigorously through her bishops on the one hand and her militant laymen and theologians on the other. In his Encyclical of March 19th, 1937, which appeared a week before another condemning Nazism, Pius XI denounced the policy of the "outstretched hand" and gave Catholics a sharp reminder of their duties on the social and economic plane.

After the second World War, as we saw in the previous chapter, the warnings of the bishops in every country in the world were exceedingly precise and firm in the context of each nation's particular situation. The decree of the Holy Office (July 1st, 1949), to the contents of which we have drawn attention above, sanctioned the decisions taken in each country.

[3] V. Joannes, "Communistes et Catholiques", *Cahiers du Communisme 6*, 1948, p. 615.

[4] V. Leduc, "Le Vatican et les princes de l'Eglise contre l'union des partisans de la paix", *Cahiers du Communisme*, 4, 1952, p. 381.

From even a brief analysis of the Communist tactic in a country like France, where Communists are not in the majority—and the same situation is found elsewhere—one fact is evident, namely, that under the pretext of advocating certain social, economic and political claims, an effort is made to win increasingly large groups of Christians over to Communism, with all that this implies.

To achieve this, Communism monopolizes the great ideals of justice, brotherhood and peace and asks the Christian masses to work with it in order to make them realities. Communists believe that common action along Communist lines is the best means of winning the wavering masses over to its side. All the more so since common action is always accompanied by Communist explanations of the situation which, little by little, will commend the justice of the Communist position to the man who is carried along by this action and, since he has no leisure, forgets to reflect upon all the suggestions that are made to him. Further, the Communist criticism of the real or imaginary weaknesses of the Church leads the Christian who listens to it without submitting it to serious examination—and this in many cases could not be undertaken—to doubt the mystery of the Church's holiness which cannot be immediately identified with that of her members, clerical or lay. At the same time Communism shakes a man's faith in the God-man, Jesus Christ, and prepares the ground for the acceptance of the Marxist concept of religion as a product of human activity caught up in and conditioned by given economic, social and political factors.

Communism achieves its purposes in liberal democratic countries within the framework of their parliamentary and trades unionist institutions, etc. It will make every effort to do the same on a permanent basis when the system of government affords it full and complete facilities, as in the People's Democracies where it is in power.

In fact, Communism pursues the same aim in the European

and Asiatic countries but under conditions and by means which differ profoundly from those it finds and uses in countries like France. It seeks to bring about the progressive disappearance of the *reality* of Christianity in the consciousness of the man who has turned Socialist.

The attitude adopted by Communism in the People's Democracies towards Christians and their Church has been frequently analysed. This attitude has varied from country to country and, from 1945 until today, according to the intensity of the religious life of the people, the rites to which they belong (Roman, Uniat, Orthodox), the position of Communism itself in each country and the reactions of foreign countries.

These attitudes and the different phases of their evolution we shall not describe again here, but it is important for our purpose to make quite clear the objectives pursued and the methods used by Communism in regard to the Christian religion wherever it has encountered it over the past fifteen years.

The aim is obvious and directly linked to the general objectives of the movement. These may be summarized as the creation of economic societies of the collectivist type on the model of what has been achieved in the Soviet Union since 1917, the creation of a new type of man entirely and finally liberated from all forms of economic, social and political oppressions and from all forms of ideology with which his consciousness is littered. In the case of Christians, more particularly, it is essential to wean them from their religious faith which is held to be one of the major obstacles to their transformation into Communists. This aim can only be realized gradually and by successive stages. Too much haste might reveal what the aim is and provoke among the population reactions which, even though stopping short of martyrdom except in a few cases, could only be detrimental to the cause. Too much delay or softness might favour the preservation of institutions and ideologies opposed to the movement towards Communism.

Christianity, it is considered, constitutes a *united* political force since all Christians belong to the Church—and Catholics in particular to the Roman Catholic Church. Hence the first task to attempt is the disintegration of this political force which is both national and international. The translation of these aims into action involves the attainment of two immediate objectives:

1. The separation of the Catholic community in a People's Democracy from the universal Catholic body.

2. The breaking down of the Catholic community within the nation into various opposing groups.

This concept of the Church as an *organized political force* is at the back of a certain number of practical attitudes which vary of course in different countries.

But this is not the end of the story. The Catholic's faith and his loyalty to the Church must be gradually destroyed. Hence campaigns aimed at undermining this Christian faith by discrediting the Church. If these are to be effective, they will have to be waged through a re-education of men's minds. As Marx-Leninist ideas suggest, the Church is not to be directly attacked, for this would undoubtedly produce the opposite of what is desired. The institutional Church must be transformed little by little in such a way that its Christian character is gradually corrupted as its members are persuaded to adopt Communist attitudes in their daily life. At the same time, so long as it survives as an institution, it cooperates in the building up of Communism. The surest way to bring about the slow death of faith is to relegate it to certain sectors of private life that become increasingly restricted, while at the same time inducing those who still call themselves Christians to act in a Marxist spirit. The Church as an institution can be an instrument which, if handled well, will contribute towards this transformation. Hence the leaders of the Christian community, bishops or priests, will be called upon to collaborate in campaigns of Communist inspiration.

The pattern of these different stages can be roughly summarized as follows:

In the first place, during an initial period varying in length from country to country, the Communist authorities behave correctly towards the Church, while from time to time inaugurating at some point or other (schools, marriage) a movement which normally involves a collision with Catholics, yet in such a way that the latter will be made to appear as a splinter group in the national community which is re-forming itself around the Communist government. Religious freedom may even be proclaimed as in China in 1949, but at the same time an indoctrination or a method of formation will be put forward and will gradually become a duty which the good citizen cannot avoid.

This period, during which psychological pressure is eased or a favourable conditioning achieved, has occurred, it would seem, in the majority of cases. It is followed by another, when the attack becomes much more intensive.

At this stage, there is above all an attempt to *discredit* the Church in the minds of the faithful and to create cracks in the edifice which, if they widened, would make it possible to ruin the unity of Catholicism everywhere. There are propaganda campaigns in which the pope is attacked as head of the Vatican State in league financially and politically with the imperialist powers. Christianity is represented as an instrument of capitalist domination or of the conquest of coloured by white peoples. Religious rites are looked on as superstitions, every form of religion is considered as a relic of a pre-scientific mentality or as opposed to the progress of the sciences. The bishops are accused of being collaborators in Vatican policy which cannot fail to oppose the genuine national interests of the various People's Democracies. A whole relevant propaganda literature complements to the full the effects of public meetings at which these themes are developed. This propaganda also denounces the Church's previous behaviour and the ways in which she is implicated in the capitalist economic system—landed property, financial holdings, etc.

Such a phase may be more or less violent, more or less lengthy according to the Catholic communities attacked. It may even scarcely exist at the beginning of the struggle. Nevertheless, it is inherent in the whole complex of relationships between Communism and Christianity, it is one of the methods by which men's minds are re-educated.

This phase is succeeded, or in some instances replaced by a period of arrests or spectacular trials of the type which were staged in the U.S.S.R. against the Catholic minority in 1922 and 1923. The arrest of Cardinal Mindszenty in Hungary in 1948 is a case in point. It is preceded by a systematic dissolution of specifically Catholic associations and groups, such as schools, charitable organizations, the Catholic press, etc. These are replaced by patriotic associations which have three advantages. They cause dissension among Catholics, between those who join them and those who are not members, whether priests or laymen. They mobilize the Catholic forces—or a large section of them at least—for common action with Communists under Communist inspiration, or else they bring about an acceptance of principles which implicitly compromise the unity of the universal Church. They see to it that the influence of the Church as an institution serves the ends pursued by the State.

The upshot of all these operations is to be the re-education of the people's minds in a Communist sense. "It must be realized", writes an eye-witness, "that if Communism wants to re-educate a man, it desires to do so completely and thoroughly. It wants to change man's whole habit of thought, his whole mentality and activity, his understanding of the meaning of life. It wants its supporters' concept of the world, their attitude of mind, the way they live and act, to be truly communist."[5] This re-education is brought about in various ways, by formative lectures, schools, meetings, self-criticism, etc. At the same time, membership of Communist-inspired movements gives practical value to the theoretical formation.

Although this pattern provides a brief summary of the essential conflict between Communism and Christianity in the People's Democracies, it is not found in its complete form in any one of them. But in each case, the factors we have indicated are found in varying proportions. In so far, too, as we do not mention the results obtained and Catholic reactions to this Communist procedure, the pattern is incomplete. But our aim here is not to describe in full the clash between Communism and Christianity but to make clear what aim is being pursued and the methods put into operation by Communism.

The indications we have just given show clearly that the objective is not a direct and open persecution of Christianity. Persecution is merely a contributory factor and only comes into play in so far as it is needed to disintegrate the Christian community in a nation under a Communist regime. The aim is to abolish the Christian faith by using ecclesiastical institutions for the purpose, after they have been reduced to silence, their evangelizing mission confined to the *private* preaching of the Gospel and to prayer within the four walls of churches and until such time as they no longer have any *raison d'être*.

At the heart of all the criticism, denunciations and campaigns is an attack on loyalty to the Church for, once that is corrupted, the faith of Christians will also subtly but surely be undermined and these men will be re-educated in the required direction. If the Church is criticized and discredited by instancing one or other of her real or imaginary compromises with capitalism, it is so that faith may be corrupted, not purified, as some may occasionally imagine.

[5] A. Michel, *Problèmes religieux dans un pays sous régime communiste*, Ed. Fleurus, Paris, 1955, p. 25.

CHRISTIANITY ON TRIAL IN THE U.S.S.R.

If we leave Catholic territory for a moment and examine the present state of the relations between Communism and Christianity in a country where the Communist regime has had forty years of expansion and growth, we shall find confirmation of the conclusion we have just drawn.

We shall leave to one side the situation of Catholics (who are in a minority in the U.S.S.R.) and that of the Orthodox Church. We shall concentrate solely on the *present* trends in the attitude of Russian Communism towards orthodox Christianity as such. We therefore leave to one side the whole history of the relations between religion and the State in the U.S.S.R. and merely point out some of the present tendencies.

For the past fifteen years or so religion has once more been tolerated in the U.S.S.R. Churches and State live together on the basis of the separation promulgated as far back as the Constitution of 1918 but not effectively applied in a peaceful manner until the last war. This does not imply any recognition of religion as such, whether Christian or Mohammedan. It is simply tolerated as a survival from the past in so far as it is expressed in and through socially organized Churches whose patriotic attitude during and since the end of the war has been appreciated by the regime, in so far, too, as it does not influence or inspire the social life of the people as a whole.

What is tolerated is public worship but within limits narrower in practice than those guaranteed by the 1936 Constitution. Religious manifestations other than those connected with public worship are not permitted in any shape or form in the U.S.S.R. If freedom of worship is recognized, it is on certain conditions. At the Council of 1945, which elected the Patriarch Alexis, the Orthodox Church was obliged to vote an ecclesiastical statute according to the terms of which the Orthodox Church accepts all the previous Soviet legislation in religious matters. This limits the external manifesta-

tions of religion to public worship alone, forbids all forms of
the apostolate that are at all organized, and restricts the
written expression of Orthodox religious thought to the publication of a small number of devotional books and to a review
intended for the Orthodox clergy, the *Review of the Moscow
Patriarchate.*

The fact of religion is only partially accepted by the rulers
of the U.S.S.R. Religion is tolerated as a survival of the capitalist past rather than recognized as a reality. This toleration
itself witnesses, it is true, to the vitality of religion as such
in the Soviet Union after forty years of persecution and
ideological warfare. That this vitality is admitted is also
evident from fragmentary details contained in the brief analysis of the religious situation found in ideological propaganda
articles and pamphlets. Nevertheless, the years of anti-
religious struggle have had widespread destructive results and
have led tens of millions of people into apostasy, irreligion
or religious indifferentism.

If during these forty years the concrete situation in regard
to religion has varied at different periods and according to
circumstances, the theoretical, ideological position as a whole
has remained unchanged. Yet a careful examination of
present-day Soviet anti-religious ideology reveals the fact that,
in relation to Karl Marx's ideas, there has been:

1. A deviation from Marx in the field of the criticism of
religion.

2. An increased loyalty to him in respect of the importance
accorded to pragmatic experience (*praxis*) in the formation
of the conscience of atheist Soviet man.

We shall now examine these two points:

1. Most of the criticisms levelled against religion in recent
pamphlets and books derives from a so-called opposition
between religion and the exact sciences, physical or natural.
These criticisms are new neither in form nor content. They
were encountered in the Western world at the time when

scientific positivism was in the ascendant and they have had a long life.

If we compare these anti-religious concepts with those enunciated by Karl Marx, we are forced to note that, in this field, the identification by Soviet ideology of Marx-Leninism with science involves the reduction of Marxism to positivism. This reduction of Marxism to positivism was inevitable once Engels had identified Marx's thought with the theses put forward in the *Anti-Dühring*, and above all when he tried to construct a dialectic of nature which would ensure complete agreement between Marxism and science at the stage it had reached in 1878 at the time Engels was writing. At the beginning of the century Lenin's controversies with the idealist philosophers were based on the scientific discoveries of that period and inevitably hastened the process.

2. Loyalty to Marx is obvious in the realm of *praxis*. This is far more serious. It manifests itself to the extent that on one hand the direct struggle against religion consisting of an attack on religious ceremonies, public worship and individuals, is relegated to a position of secondary importance, though this does not mean that pressure is not brought to bear in one or other of these sectors; on the other hand, it is assumed that general and active cooperation in the building up of Socialism will eliminate from the consciousness of the masses religious beliefs and the religious sense. It is assumed that the exciting adventure of progress towards Communism will convince men of man's dominion over nature. The development of great public works in the Soviet Union, the loudly trumpeted claim that men in the Soviet Union are responsible for all the great scientific and technical discoveries which have improved and are still improving the lot of humanity—a claim the West derides without grasping its full import—give colour among the Soviet masses to the view that the Russian Communist is truly the demiurge of a universe which he creates and transforms within the framework

of the "objective laws" of science. He is that "true man" of the new era—whom Marx glimpsed in some of his notes which, though unpublished, are of great importance in determining the bases of his thought. The new era is that of "Communism which, in so far as it is integral naturalism, is humanism, and in so far as it is integral humanism, is naturalism."

Since Soviet anti-religious ideology is more solidly knit to the central theses of Karl Marx, it can more easily adapt itself to a genuine tolerance of those Churches which canalize the religious faith of believers and so keep within bounds its anarchic and explosive manifestations so frequent for centuries past in Russia. Further, it is no longer so much a question of directly attacking beliefs as of forming the conscience of this "true man". In practice, this means the consciences of those young men who are the hope of the future. It is obvious that the directives given to the Komsomol of recent years in articles published in the *Molodoi Kommunist*, are both farseeing and faithful to Marx's conception of the part played by pragmatic experience (*praxis*) in the formation of a conscience emerging from the very process by which man produces his own life. It is by making men *act* that we shall form consciences with a collective sense. Then, by inculcating the *idea* of the sovereign value of science, we shall prepare them to accept the conclusions of Marxism, the only true science, in every department of life. "All social life is essentially *practical*", wrote Karl Marx, "all the mysteries which urge theory towards mysticism find their rational solution in pragmatic experience (*praxis*) and in the interpretation of this experience."

The emphasis laid on the importance of collective action for the elimination of the "relics of capitalism" shows that the Soviets rely as much, if not more, on the formation of a new awareness in young people as on the pseudo-scientific criticism of religion, in order to create this "true" and radically atheist man who, in Marx's view, would be the type of Communist humanity. We may ask whether this method would be as fruitful were loyalty to Marxism chiefly secured by *acceptance* of a form of scientific positivism. We may wonder whether, at the level of propaganda publications, Marxism does not reduce itself or tend to reduce itself to just that. If such an attitude became general, might it not produce a serious cleavage in men's consciences when this positivism is clearly seen to be inadequate? If the Russian consciousness as a whole began to question its value, as the secularized Western consciousness has questioned it and still continues to do so, what would happen? Certain facts denounced by the *Komsomolskaya Pravda* concern the revival of faith among young Communists who have completed their technical studies at grammar school level. Do they not show that the problem exists? But at both the theoretical and the practical levels the Party keeps a watchful eye on all that is happening in the area of those "relics of capitalism" which it holds the religious sense and religion itself to be.

Today, as in the recent past, Marx-Leninism involves the same fight against God and all that reminds man of God. It is an effort "to recast and reconstruct the human world of thought and the whole human scale of values in terms of this state of war against God" (J. Maritain). It offers itself as the total solution of the total human problem. "It desires to dominate the whole of existence, not merely some of its moments" (N. Berdyaev). It claims to be not only a social or economic but an integral human phenomenon.

CHAPTER III

WHAT IS COMMUNISM?

Our study of the decisions of the Magisterium has shown
that as and when the Church finds herself at grips with Communism she recognizes it as radically opposed to herself in
every detail of what it involves, and she rejects it for many
reasons of which the most fundamental is that it is an
atheistic, anti-Christian doctrine.

But we may be tempted to ask whether in so doing the
Church is not exaggerating one of the characteristics of
modern Communism founded as it is on Marx-Leninist doctrine.[1] Is not Marxism above all a doctrine, a "guide for
action" in the sphere of politics, economics and the social
system? Is not its aim the transformation of the various forms
of society? Could we not go so far as to say that it is a
sociology engaged in analysing the fundamental functional
elements of these societies and laying bare their real structures?

More than one Marxist author, Communist or otherwise,

[1] Since Christians are confronted essentially by Marxism as understood by Lenin, Stalin and the Soviet and foreign Communists who
claim kinship with the Third International, it is principally with this
form of Marxism, i.e. Marx-Leninism, that we shall deal here. And
we shall return to the sources—Marx and Engels—whenever necessary. This does not mean that we are unaware of other interpretations
such as those of E. Bernstein, K. Kautsky, Bukharin, Lukacs, etc.,
and other Marxist movements, e.g. certain types of Socialism and
Trotskyism. But we shall not deal with them here, even when we use
the term "Marxism" without any other qualification.

may be brought forward to give evidence in favour of this view. Yet these witnesses would be disloyal to Karl Marx and F. Engels, the founders of that "scientific Socialism" whose ultimate stage of development is to be Communism. Nor would they be faithful to Lenin, the first politician to attempt to inscribe upon human history the lineaments of a Communist regime inspired by Marxism.

Lenin rightly notes that "by deepening and developing philosophical materialism, Marx brought it to its logical conclusion and enlarged its field to include knowledge of *human society* in addition to knowledge of nature". The Marxism on which modern Communism is based is a world view and implies both a *philosophy* and a *plan of action*. The *Archives de Philosophie* rightly wrote in 1939: "Marxism is not only a method, a programme of government, a technical solution of economic problems, still less a fluctuating opportunism or a theme for oratorical ranting. It offers itself as an over-all view of man and of history, of the individual and of society, of nature and of God."[2]

After stating the essential themes of Marxist philosophy, we shall briefly examine Marxist sociology and Marx-Leninist political doctrine.

MARXIST PHILOSOPHY

Karl Marx's thought differs from every other system in an *apparent* absence of any dogmatic statement concerning a mass of problems which are treated no longer in isolation from one another, e.g. matter, the theory of knowledge, nature, man, etc. Each of these problems is examined within a given historical, social, political and economic context.

In his *Theses on Feuerbach*, which sum up Marx's conclusions after his first ten years of reflection (1837–46), man does not grasp abstract objects in order to know them and

[2] *Archives de Philosophie*, Vol. XV, book II, Beauchesne, Paris, 1939, p. 1.

then to transform them. He takes his place in the emergent process of his relations with nature and grasps these objects by means of social action (*praxis*) which knows things as it produces them, while at the same time man by means of this action produces himself.

Following Ludwig Feuerbach, Karl Marx explains man in terms of his needs. "Man", he wrote in the *Economic and Philosophical Manuscripts of 1844*, "is a *natural* being. As a natural being, as a living natural being, he is endowed on the one hand with *natural powers*, with *vital powers* ... ; these powers exist in him under the form of aptitudes and instincts. On the other hand, is so far as he is an objective, natural, corporal, sensitive being, he is a being who *suffers*; he is dependent and limited, that is, the objects of his instincts exist outside him, are independent of him, yet they are the objects he *needs*, they are indispensable and essential if his inherent powers are to be actuated and ratified."

The starting point of human history is therefore the living man seeking to satisfy a certain number of primordial needs in order to live. "The primary historical fact is the production of the means which enable these needs to be satisfied." But once they are satisfied, the way is open for new needs.

Man's behaviour is essentially an argument, a struggle with nature which has to provide him with the means of satisfying his need to drink, to eat, to clothe himself, to develop his powers and then his intellectual and artistic capacities. In this long and difficult enterprise, man discovers himself as a productive being who becomes human through his work. He discovers too that he is a creative activity taking possession of nature and appropriating it to the full in his work, provided that he is truly man, that is, man in society and that member of a social species whom Karl Marx always has in mind when he uses the word "man". Man humanizes nature and at the same time makes himself natural. In other words, by his creative activity and by his work, he brings about his own identity with nature which he masters. He has emerged from nature and by his opposition to her, achieves his own total evolution. Man is at first crushed by nature, but through his struggle with her he becomes aware of what separates him from her and finds in her the conditions required for his own fulfilment, for the achievement of his own true stature as man. This awareness and this struggle are inseparable, they are at the heart of the Marxist concept of man. By taking possession of the whole range of creative activities, man discovers that "all we call history is nothing but the process of man's creation through human work, nothing but the evolution of nature in the human field. He has therefore an evident and irrefutable proof that he is his own creator."

Beyond himself and nature, man discovers nothing. His awareness of human activity in this universal dimension reveals to him that "for man, the supreme being is man". God, creation, metaphysical problems are therefore so many empty words. When man becomes fully natural, he sees himself clearly for what he is, for he has been made aware of man in his totality as the human species. His work has shown him that he cannot act, cannot develop except within the human species as a whole. It has shown him that he is a social being, a *Gattungswesen*, as Marx puts it, and nothing else. Towards the end of his life F. Engels wrote that work "is the fundamental primary condition of all human life, so much so that there is a sense in which work must be said to have created man himself". He cannot be created by anyone else, by a God. "Karl Marx's atheism", wrote Jean Lacroix in *Esprit*, "is the direct outcome of his definition of man as a being who is *essentially a worker* achieving his own status by transforming the world through his work."

Man according to Marx is therefore a self-sufficient being, an atheistic being, a being without God. He develops *only* through his relationship with that "other" which he bears within himself—nature.

This is not the place to inquire how this radically atheistic concept of man is the development of L. Feuerbach's ideas and the adoption, in a context emptied of all references to man's spiritual activity, of one of the central concepts in the German philosopher G. W. F. Hegel's *Phenomenology of Mind.* We merely take note of the radical atheism at the basis of Karl Marx's view of man. "Atheism is not a structure imposed upon Marxism, it is absolutely essential to it" (J. Lacroix).

Man produces and, by producing in community, creates values through his work and through it alone. And these values, once created, are assessed only in relation to the quantity of human work expended in their production. But in the actual world in which man lives, the values he has created to satisfy his human needs fall from his grasp. They take concrete form in goods, money and ultimately in capital. These exist *apart from* all the mutual human relationships established by men in their productive activity. The product of human labour achieved through processes that are increasingly *social* as man's power over nature develops, becomes the *private* property of certain men because of an initial aggression of man against his fellows.

Hence, the products of man's labour as he transforms nature lose their character as human products and finally become fetishes, that is, agents of oppression to which the man who owns them as his *private* property and the man from whom they have been taken both submit. All men, whether capitalists or proletarians, ultimately find themselves deprived of the reality which increased their human stature —their dialectical link with nature—the capitalists because they *selfishly* enjoy the goods which they have appropriated to themselves as individuals, the rest because they are denied these goods. There ensues a domination of man over man, a transfer of the power of man over nature to the power of man over his neighbour, which makes impossible the oneness of man with nature and his oneness with himself. The dialectical link with nature which made man what he *essentially* is, is severed, and man is incapable of achieving his universal essence in this world of private property.

In his relationships with the fetishes to which he submits and consequently in his relationships with other men, man is conscious of himself as being torn from himself, a being who has lost himself, a creature despoiled and naked. This is the relationship Marx calls exploitation. Under the regime of *private*, individualist appropriation of goods, man is an exploited being who has lost his original freedom.

This exploitation of man has therefore as its foundation the *private*, individualist appropriation of goods produced by man's *social* activity. It is a *real* exploitation, for man is despoiled of what makes him man—his creative activity through which he transforms nature. It attains its full dimensions in the capitalist system in which a considerable portion of the value of the goods produced by the worker is taken from him and transformed into a *surplus-value*. This the capitalist appropriates *privately* as he does the rest. As it accumulates, it furthers the development of the system. It is only when man, despoiled, exploited and lost, has realized that his loss and his exploitation place him everywhere in an inhuman situation—and this, according to Marx, is the situation of the proletarian—that, taking advantage of the machinery of social self-destruction (namely, the crises which the capitalist system involves) he will bring about a radical transformation of his situation by means of a revolution. The revolution will be the prelude to the inauguration of Communism and the restoration of the reign of freedom. "Instead of the old bourgeois society with its classes and its class antagonisms, there will be substituted a society of men in which the free development of all depends on the free development of each."

Meanwhile, fundamental economic exploitation gives rise

to political and ideological exploitations whose purpose is to offer a falsified picture and an illusory justification of the counterfeit world in which relationships between man and man are perverted as a result of the perversion of the dialectical relationships between man and nature.

The concept of man as a being who is *nothing but* a producer allowed Karl Marx to account for economic exploitation, for the loss man sustains in his economic life when the goods he manufactures become private property. This same concept makes it possible to explain why and how a fundamental economic exploitation is inevitably accompanied by secondary and, for the most part, ideological exploitations.

Placed as he is at the summit of the scale of living beings in the order of nature, man, absolutely self-sufficient, appears as the term of a long biological and historical process which owes its meaning to the fact that it has produced man. Man emerges from within his struggle with nature just as self-awareness emerges in the dialectic of the master and the slave in Hegel's *Phenomenology of Mind*. But "here, in direct contrast to German philosophy which comes down from heaven to earth, we rise from earth to heaven", wrote Karl Marx in 1846.

By accepting a complex of social relationships, and as a result of work done in common, men form their consciousness and their liberty. It is a fact that "specific individuals, actively productive in a specific way, assent to specific social and political relationships". The ideas and the mental images which they form are *immediately* implicit in their material activity and their material relations: "the act of representing men's mutual spiritual intercourse to the imagination and the mind, appears as the direct emanation of their material relationship." And, Marx continues, the same is true for every spiritual activity, whether in the field of politics, law, morals and metaphysics or in that of religion. "Men are producers of their own mental images, their own ideas, but only if they are real, active men with the specific formation they receive from a specific development of their productive powers." Morals, metaphysics, religion have no history, but "men who develop their material productivity become more real and efficient and at the same time alter their way of thinking and its products". In other words, Marx concludes, "it is not consciousness which determines life, it is life which determines consciousness".

At the beginning of his career, Karl Marx analysed briefly the political exploitation of man in the bourgeois State whether monarchical (even in a parliamentary form) or republican. In it man finds himself divided against himself. He is both a citizen and an economic man, a social being in the political community (in theory at least) and a private individual in his economic life where he is a means to an end, dominated by the external power of economic fetishes. The bourgeois State thus becomes the instrument of the domination of the propertied classes over the others. If this is so, it is because there is "a connection between the social and political structure and production", a connection which must be laid bare by any analysis that penetrates the fog of mystification. "The social structure and the State continually emerge from the vital evolution of specific individuals . . . as they *really* are, that is, as they act and produce in the material sphere."

There are various forms of ideological exploitation—economic and juridical theories justifying the economic and social system. Karl Marx examines the former at length in *Capital*, the latter in *German Ideology* (1846) which was published posthumously. But ideological exploitation reaches its extreme expression in religion which is none other than its most subtle form.

Karl Marx adopted as his own the ideas on the nature of religion worked out in left-wing Hegelian circles after Hegel's death, and the theory developed by Ludwig Feuerbach. He considers as definitely established the proposition "Man

makes religion, it is not religion which makes man". Religion
is a *product* of the consciousness of man contained within a
certain conditioning pattern, social, political and economic.
It is that and *nothing else*. It is the *reflection* in consciousness
of the situation of a man who "either has not found himself
(primitive man) or who has already lost himself again (man in
the world of private property)". It is the reflection of the real
world of private property in the consciousness of exploited
man who cannot achieve his own universal essence in this
world. "It is the imaginary achievement of the essence of
man, because in it the essence of man has no genuine reality."
In a world where man is oppressed by money, by capital,
"religion is the sigh of the creature overwhelmed by mis-
fortune, the soul of a heartless world, just as it is the spirit
of a spiritless age. It is an opium for the people." Lenin said
the same a few years before the Russian Revolution of 1917.

This being so, religion must be suppressed, since it is "the
illusory sun that revolves about man, for so long as he does
not revolve about himself". This is a return to and the putting
into practice of the fundamental concept of man according to
Marx and his successors—man is a godless being. In the end
there must be an "absolutely positive suppression of religion",
for all those social conditions in which a man is a being "de-
based, enslaved, abandoned, despicable" must be done away
with. Religion is one of these social conditions. But since
religion is an ideological exploitation that is a reflection of
economic exploitation, it is by suppressing the latter or, more
exactly, the conditions produced by it, that success will be
achieved. The best way to suppress religion is to fight the
capitalist regime and to recruit even believers for the struggle.
As Lenin pointed out, such action will have far more effect on
these than any speeches or anti-religious demonstrations.

By her increasing emphasis on the atheism of Communism
in her stand against it, the Catholic Church shows her profound insight. Atheism is at the heart of the concept of

Marxist man—man who, in the end, is made one with nature
in Communism. The sociology developed by Marxism is to a
great extent the application of this concept to the analysis of
the social and economic structures of modern society. Similarly Marxist politics is an effort to find ways and means of
bringing to the world of today an economic and social structure in which this concept will eventually find concrete
expression.

MARXIST SOCIOLOGY

Many Marx-Leninist Communists would now deny that
Marxism is a sociology. Yet Lenin recognized that the hypothesis which serves as the basis of the Marxist analyses has
one merit: "it made possible, for the first time, a *scientific*
sociology".[3] This hypothesis was formulated by Karl Marx in
1859 in the Preface to his *Critique of Political Economy*. The
main "thread" running through these studies "may be briefly
defined as follows":

> As they produce the social conditions of their existence, men
> enter into specific, necessary relationships whether they wish to
> or not, relationships in the field of production which corre-
> spond to a specific degree of development reached by their
> productive powers in the material sphere. The sum total of
> these relationships in the field of production constitutes the
> economic structure of society, the concrete basis on which
> rises a juridical and political superstructure, and to which
> correspond specific forms of social consciousness. The mode
> of production of the material needs of life conditions the
> development of social, political and intellectual life in general.
> It is not men's consciousness which determines their being; on
> the contrary, it is their social being which determines their
> consciousness.[4]

[3] Lenin, *Who are these "Friends of the People?" and how do they
combat the Social-Democrats?*
[4] K. Marx, *Critique of Political Economy*.

This hypothesis, raised to the level of a method and a principle which explains society, has since been given the name of *historical materialism*. Karl Marx applies it to the analysis which he makes of capitalist society in the *Communist Manifesto* (1848) and in *Capital* (1867) as well as in other writings in which he studies the society of his own times—for instance, in the articles collected under the title *Class Struggles in France* or the pamphlet *The 18th of Brumaire of Louis-Napoleon*. But the analyses in the last two works are in general less systematic than those of the *Communist Manifesto*, as F. Engels already noted in a letter to Joseph Bloch dated September 21st, 1890. Although he had been reflecting upon it for a considerable number of years, Marx did not formulate his hypothesis of work in rigid terms. In the German text of the Preface, different expressions are used to indicate identical realities. There is therefore no reason why the concepts he employs in his analysis of human societies should be too strictly defined.

The obvious sense of Marx's text is that the real structure of society is the following:

1. The true basis of society or its economic structure (sometimes called in current usage its substructure). This economic structure includes:

(a) the "material productive forces",

(b) the "production relationships", taken as a whole.

"The production relationships in every society", he wrote in *Poverty of Philosophy* (1847), "form a complete whole."

These two are linked together. "Specific, necessary production relationships" correspond to a certain degree of development in the former. As Karl Marx does not explain the nature of this correspondence in the Preface, divergent interpretations arise in subsequent Marxism.

Further, the distinction between productive forces and the production relationships is not clearly elucidated by Marx nor by later Marxists. Must natural conditions be included in the productive forces or not? Are techniques part of the productive forces, or of the production relationships? They are just as much the result of scientific knowledge and of the organization and division of labour as of the productive forces put into operation.

2. Over against the economic structure stands the superstructure. This superstructure has a juridical and a political character.

3. To this same economic structure correspond "specific social forms of consciousness". Of the nature of the correspondence between the ideological forms and the economic structure Karl Marx has nothing to say in this work, except that they are the forms in which men become aware of the conflict arising within the economic structure between the material productive forces and the existing production relationships expressed in the juridical property relationships.

In order to clarify Marx's ideas concerning the mutual relationships arising from the three categories "economic structure", "superstructure" and "ideology", we must return to his *German Ideology* (1846) to which he refers explicitly in the 1859 Preface.

Originally there are real men who produce their own life and reproduce it by enlarging its scope. Therefore the forces of material production are basic.

To produce and reproduce this life, men enter into "specific social and political relationships" of which the family is the initial type.

Hence "to produce life—one's own through one's work as well as that of others by procreation—now seems to imply a kind of double relationship. On the one hand there is a kind of natural relationship, on the other a kind of social relationship." Marx at once makes it clear in what sense "social relationship" is to be understood—"social in the sense that by the term is understood the joint action of several individuals", social therefore in the sense that men cooperate

with one another in their work. Marx, like his contemporary
Proudhon, is impressed by the forces which cooperation rep-
resents at a given stage of industrial evolution. While Proudhon speaks of "collective forces", Marx puts the mode of
cooperation on the same footing as a "productive force". It
is at this point that we perceive the link which allows Marx
to include in the economic structure the "real basis" of
society, the social relationships that men establish with each
other. All the more so since, in his view, "the mass of productive forces available to men determines social conditions"
and so is at the basis of society. "The social structure and the
State are always the result of the life process of specific
individuals . . . as they are *in reality*, that is, as they work
and produce material things." The political relationships
which men establish among themselves depend on material
production and its form. The same is true of their juridical
relationships.

The economic factor is therefore primordial and essential
in Marx's thought. In it the political factor has its origin and
to it the social factor is reducible. It is this reduction of the
social to the economic factor which vitiates the whole of
Marx's analysis. It is no mere accident; we find it in *Capital*
as well as in *German Ideology* and the *Economic and Philosophical Manuscripts of 1844*.

The forms taken by the social consciousness—ideas, mental
images, etc.—to the extent that they are "the language of
real life", are products of the economic activity of men who
are "real, active, and conditioned by a specific development
of their productive forces and by the relationships corresponding to these". The politics, law, morality and religion of a
nation are "the direct emanation of their behaviour in the
material sphere". They, like the juridical, political superstructure, arise from the real foundation of society, and if
they become ideologies, the reason will be found in "the
historical process of human life".

According to Lenin, who described the introduction of "the idea of materialism into sociology" by Marx as a "stroke of genius", the conclusions reached by Marx are of interest from three points of view:

1. They make it possible to invalidate the conclusion that "social relationships have been consciously established by men". This, he says, "is completely contradicted by all the historical evidence". By extending the anlysis to the very origins of man's social ideas, Karl Marx has abolished this contradiction.

2. By bringing to the forefront "a perfectly objective criterion resulting from the discovery that the production relationships are the structure of society", historical materialism has made it possible to apply to these relationships "the general scientific criterion of recurrence". The analysis of these relationships has made it possible to observe the regular recurrence of the same phenomena in various social regimes and so also to work out a fundamental concept, that of "an economic social formation".

3. Finally, "by reducing social relationships to the production relationships and the latter to the level of the productive forces, a solid basis has been given to the view that the development of social structures is a process in the field of natural history".[5] In the speech which F. Engels made at Marx's funeral in 1883, he declared that this was Karl Marx's claim to glory.

Thus Lenin emphasizes a concept proper to Karl Marx, which describes human society in its totality—the concept of *economic social formation*. All human society then appears as the sum total of a mass of complex relationships which can only be distinguished from one another by a process of abstraction—*economic* relationships which indicate man's relationships with nature, *social* relationships which indicate men's relationships with one another. "The economic factor,

[5] Lenin, *op. cit.*

that is, the productive forces, includes natural elements (the earth and its resources, climate, the biological data proper to a given human group, etc.) and elements that are specifically human, practical, the fruits of the historical struggle, and which transform these natural data—techniques, instruments, knowledge, organization", as Henri Lefebvre explains. "Yet", he continues, "the social relationships have their own specific character and their own inner contradictions. They are, at one and the same time, relationships of association and of domination, of practical solidarity and of competition, of solidarity and of exploitation. And this is true of the most simple and the most complex, of the relationships between the sexes and the relationships between classes."[6]

To return to Karl Marx: the totality of human society, conceived as an economic and social formation, appears to be in process of becoming. "Roughly speaking", he wrote in the Preface to the *Critique of Political Economy*, "the Asiatic, ancient, feudal and modern forms of bourgeois production may be *called* progressive stages of economic social formation." We note in passing the vague sense of the word "called" in this sentence, in which the great "moments" of history, according to Hegel's conception of its evolution in his *Lectures on the Philosophy of History*, are transferred to the economic plane.

This method, this historical materialism, these concepts were worked out by Karl Marx in *Capital* when he analysed the capitalist regime. He analysed the mercantile economic system, its functioning and its development, in his effort to bring to light the real nature of the production relationships which are established between men in capitalist society.

It is chiefly from the "classical" English economists, Adam Smith and David Ricardo, that he borrowed the economic categories of production, consumption, social labour, the

[6] H. Lefebvre, *Problèmes actuels du communisme*, Paris, 1958, pp. 68 and 69.

division of labour, value in exchange and value in use, price, profit, wages, revenue, ground rent. But at the same time he re-shapes them and even introduces new concepts such as that of surplus-value, by which he explains profit in the capitalist system.

His whole analysis of the capitalist system is founded on the statement that man is a productive being producing his own life and his own needs by constantly expanding them, so that there is no value other than the labour of man. Marx's intuition is a simple one. He explained it clearly in a letter to his friend Kugelman. Every society in which men stop working and producing is doomed to decline and die. This intuition is similar to that developed by Saint-Simon in his parable in *l'Organisateur* (1819). Work is at the basis of every human society. This view is expressed in the assertion that value resides wholly and entirely in work.

But in bourgeois society where the capitalist appropriates to himself as a private individual the means of production and the fruit of the labourer's work, the proletarian is de-spoiled of that part of his work corresponding to the surplus-value. If this were not so, the labourer's work would not be productive in the eyes of his capitalist employer nor would it have any interest whatsoever for him. Karl Marx is not concerned to discover whether in capitalist society there are sources of surplus-value other than the exploitation of human labour. The important thing is to have revealed this particular source since eventually the others can be derived from it alone. He keeps on the track of the transformation of this surplus-value into profit by studying capitalism as a complex whole developing in a context of inevitable contradictions, namely the crises in which it is involved, and by an ever increasing exploitation of the proletarian. Thus the equili-brium of the system appears precarious, dominated as it is by the internal pressures of its own growth which are due to the more or less violent contradiction between the appropriation for private use of the products of man's activity and the social character of this productive activity. This instability is increased by the formation of a despoiled and exploited proletariat which becomes aware of its dehumanized situation and will do anything to change it by overthrowing the established order.

Fundamentally two classes oppose one another under the capitalist regime—the bourgeois class and the proletariat. Around these cluster less important classes. The class struggle which has existed since the dawn of human history now becomes acute. "The bourgeoisie produces its own grave-diggers. The ruin of the bourgeoisie and the victory of the proletariat are equally inevitable", wrote Karl Marx at the end of the first chapter of the *Communist Manifesto*, for "the bourgeois production relationships are the final form taken by that process of social production in which a contradiction is inherent. This contradiction is not an individual one, it arises from the social conditions in which individuals live. Yet at the same time, the productive forces developing within bourgeois society create the material conditions required to resolve this contradiction. This social formation therefore marks the end of human society's pre-history."

Karl Marx inherited the notion of class and class struggle from utopian Socialism and Saint-Simonism. Moreover, the work of French historians such as A. Thiers and Guizot on the French Revolution of 1789, confirms socialist ideas concerning the class struggle. Karl Marx acknowledges his debt to these men when he disclaims any kinship with Auguste Comte's theories. But he differs from the French historians in that he seems to consider the class struggle as the essential fact in social evolution. "The whole history of human society until our own times is the history of struggles between classes", he wrote at the beginning of the *Communist*

Manifesto. His successors went a little further and did not
find it at all difficult to consider the class struggle as the
ultimate principle and motive force of human history.

His concept of the last phase of the class struggle as expressed in the *Communist Manifesto* is twofold. A similar
ambiguity is also apparent in *Capital.* The revolution which is
its culminating point is in Marx's view:

1. A social phenomenon of catastrophic suddenness and
short duration, "a violent overthrow of the former conditions
of production" at the moment when the opposition between
the bourgeois class and the proletariat has reached its climax.
This concept is expounded dialectically on the model of the
Hegelian dialectic of the master and slave, in *The Holy
Family* (1845) and is akin to the ideas of Babeuf advocated
by *La fédération des bannis* ("Federation of the Banished").
It is possible that F. Engels took it from these Communists
who had sought asylum in London and he may have passed
it on to Marx.

2. A permanent revolution, in accordance with the ideas of
A. Blanqui, a temporary coalition of the proletariat and the
lower middle class in revolt against a developing capitalism
which apparently consolidates its position in the process.
Once the coalition has a majority on its side, an unofficial
proletarian force will be constituted and will take its place
side by side with the middle class revolutionary authority.
Its mission will be to undertake the long and slow political
education of the proletariat. This will gradually bring about
the transfer of legal authority from the bourgeoisie in revolt to
the revolutionary proletariat. At this point, the rise to power
of the working class has to be delayed over a long period.

Those who read the *Communist Manifesto* carefully without allowing themselves to be influenced by the brilliant and
vigorous formulas to be found throughout the first chapter,
will find some uncertainty in the thought and in the ideas,
which shows that Marx had not reconciled the concept of

the revolution as sudden and catastrophic with that of the revolution as permanent.

The category of "social class" which is essential in an analysis of the social relationships which men maintain among one another, was not analysed rigorously enough by Marx. Sometimes he understands it as meaning an "order", an "estate" in the sense of the three orders which constituted French society before the Revolution of 1789. Sometimes he understands it in a more restricted sense according to which economic realities (conditions, interests), intellectual realities (culture) and those of politics (national solidarity, political organization) play an important part in the constitution of the social class. Economic realities, and especially the place of a class in the processes of production and distribution, play a preponderant rôle in this analysis of the social class (its share in production, in distribution). The growth of awareness is also an important element in class formation. The proletariat becomes a class only when it becomes conscious of the solidarity which unites its members, and of the economic and social status which is their lot.

The social classes are considered by Marx, Lenin and Lukacs as "total social phenomena". But neither Marx nor his successors studied the social class as a specific group opposed to other human groups (economic associations, mutual insurance societies, families, non-profit-making companies, etc.) as well as to the other classes. Marx and the Marxists see the social class as opposed on the one hand to the State, and on the other, to the political party, but only to note that both State and party have a close relationship to the social class. They are a means to domination or a weapon in the struggle of one class against the others.

But class consciousness hesitates between a *real* awareness which is both individual and at the same time collective, and a consciousness labouring under *the illusion* that social relationships are the opposite of what in fact they really are.

Finally, it is a truism to observe that Karl Marx could not make up his mind as to how many social classes there are, nor whether there is or is not evidence to prove that they exist in societies other than the capitalist. Marxist sociologists still have doubts on these precise points. They often confuse the social class with the groups which form the various strata of society.

The importance attached by Marx to the social class's rôle in production as specifying it and distinguishing it from any other, is only the expression on the sociological plane of the fundamental idea that man is *essentially* and by nature a productive agent and nothing more. And it prevents Marx and later Marxism from developing whatever truth there might be in the analyses begun more than a century ago, and at the same time from providing a true analysis of the social realities of the present day.

THE POLITICAL THEORY OF MARX-LENINISM

In one of its aspects, Marxism presents itself as a political theory. This is because it is a world view, not a philosophy only but also a "praxis", a form of action. It sets out to be a "guide for action" to man in society, influencing society as it is today. The Marxist political theory issues directly from its sociology, from the philosophy of history which emerges as soon as every economic system is viewed as one of the phases in the evolution of that "social and economic formation" in which the whole of society is included.

But it is also the point at which Marxism becomes a dogmatic system under the pressure of facts which show that no given society can be built from nothing by means of a complex of concepts, however well formulated these may be.

No more than twenty years were needed to effect this transformation, which changed Marx-Leninism from an analysis of situations as Lenin understood it before and at the beginning of the 1917 Revolution in Russia, into a collection of

practical prescriptions drawn up by Stalin. And if there is to
be a genuine return to the sources, much more is required
than the "return to Leninism" as preached in the U.S.S.R.
today at the bidding of N. S. Khrushchev. An analysis of the
category "politics" would be needed in its relations to economic and social factors. It was never completed by Marx
or Lenin.

According to F. Engels, who dealt with the origin and the
nature of the State at much greater length than Marx, this
political organ of human society has not always existed. It
came on the scene only when, as a consequence of the division
of labour and the organization of a system of private property,
social classes arose with opposing interests which gave birth
to social stresses. With the establishment of the State, these
disputes were settled and confined within the economic
sphere. But at the same time the ruling class took possession
of the State and made it serve its particular interests instead
of the common weal. In the hands of these men, the State
became an instrument of domination and repression.

Hence the State is superior to society in appearance only.
This became possible only because society was divided into
opposing classes. But in fact, the State is merely an outward
expression of what society really is. It embodies and sanctions
society's class structure and in particular its domination by
one class. But it exercises this *biased* power under cover of
the reigning ideology which describes the State as an independent and impartial arbitrator, whereas it is nothing of the
kind.

Just as the State became a historical fact in the "social and
economic formation" at a given stage of its development, so
too it will disappear from it at another period when the
opposition between the classes has been surmounted by the
Revolution.

Neither Marx nor Engels gave a clear account of how this
was to be brought about. In the writings collected under the

title of *Critique of the Gotha Programme*, they even put forward points of view that are hard to reconcile with one another, as Lenin noted in 1917 shortly before the February Revolution in Russia. Lenin overcame this difficulty by introducing the notion of the proletarian State which will replace the bourgeois State once the dictatorship of the proletariat has established a socialist regime. And this proletarian State will itself dwindle away as the regime moves forward towards Communism.

In fact, the proletarian State in the U.S.S.R. has not begun to dwindle away. As the "socialist" regime develops there, the State grows stronger and arrogates to itself new powers which the bourgeois State did not possess. Its disappearance is finally considered contingent no longer upon the fulfilment of a certain number of economic conditions but on that of certain political requirements. The doctrine of the disappearance of the State under a communist regime as developed by Stalin in 1939, is the exact antithesis of the ideas put forward by Marx and Engels in both the *Communist Manifesto* and the *Critique of the Gotha Programme* (1875). The socialist State "will not survive, it will die if capitalist encirclement is done away with and replaced by socialist encirclement", Stalin declared.

Once political conditions control the evolution of one of the elements in "socialist" society, the *objective* dualism, political force-economic force, takes the place of Karl Marx's *subjective* economic-social dialectic.

Marx-Leninist politics are then obliged to neglect the negative element remaining in the Marxist dialectic of the *Communist Manifesto* and to replace it by a new idea entirely foreign to it, namely that of "death and birth". In 1938 in a book which was to become the bible, the manual for the active formation of the militant Communist in every country in the world, Stalin wrote:

If it is true that the disappearance of the old and the birth of the new is a law of growth, it is clear . . . hence, action must be based not on the social strata which are no longer evolving but on the social strata which are developing and have a future, even if for the time being they do not represent the dominating power . . . hence, to avoid mistakes in politics, we must look to the future, not to the past . . . hence, to avoid mistakes in politics, we must be revolutionaries, not reformists . . . hence, to avoid mistakes in politics, we must pursue uncompromisingly proletarian politics.[7]

These are the rules for action in Communist politics. They are sometimes set out in slightly different form. For instance, in a pamphlet entitled *The Politics of the Party* (1944), the French Communist Party gave as its permanent "rules for action":

1. It is important to determine correctly who is our chief enemy and where the main attack is to be launched (e.g. Fascism in 1934).

2. The right time must be chosen.

3. Slogans must be chosen.

4. The masses learn from their own experience.

5. We must learn to sense by what problems the people are preoccupied at any given moment.

6. Victory will not come through the avant-garde alone.

The logical application of general, abstract plans makes possible the solution of every problem. Such a method, such a "guide for action" leads to the acceptance of circumstances as they are, of empirical facts considered as the outward sign of rational reality. According to whether one is dealing with the Soviet Union or with Communism in non-Communist countries, it is either the State and its head or the Communist Party (or rather its leaders) which set themselves up as the criterion of what is real and true.

To all intents and purposes we find the same principle

[7] J. Stalin, *Dialectical and historical Materialism.*

at the basis of the politics of international Communism, especially after the death of Lenin. He had founded the alliance between the proletarian revolutionary movement and the colonial revolutionary movements of bourgeois inspiration, on an analysis (very questionable in more ways than one) of the relationships established between colonizing countries and their colonial territories during the period of growth of international financial capitalism, that is, during the period of "imperialism". But, as the U.S.S.R. consolidated its domination over the Third International (Komintern), non-economic factors played an increasingly preponderant rôle, especially the identification of the interests of the international revolutionary movement with those of the Soviet Union.

In 1936 Stalin, when presenting the proposed Constitution of the Soviet Union, solemnly proclaimed this identity. "The Constitution", he said, "will be a document witnessing to the fact that what millions of honest men in capitalist countries have dreamed of and still continue to dream of, has already been realized in the U.S.S.R." It is therefore the Soviet Union which is the criterion of the authenticity of international proletarian politics. Once again Communist politics bow to the empirical.

It makes no difference that this concept of Marx-Leninist politics was, as has been shown, contained in germ long before Marx-Leninism in Stalin's little known pamphlet *Anarchism and Socialism*. Marx-Leninist politics is not scientific politics still less a political science. It is politics founded on an empirical analysis and on a philosophy of progress akin to that of the eighteenth-century Encyclopedists.

It is the Communist Party whose mission it is to put into practice the Marx-Leninist policy decided upon by the leaders of the movement in so-called socialist countries as well as in the others. The Party is constituted as a combat force with a strong and centralized hierarchical organization. It is made up of a minority of the citizens, whether proletarian or not, which attempts by means of the appropriate slogans to enrol for its campaigns masses of men who are more or less in sympathy with it. It is convinced that by this procedure it will gradually instil Communist reactions in those who cooperate in a course of action conducted in the spirit of Marx-Leninism.

When favourable conditions have been established, the Party will lead the masses, whose backbone it is, in the attack upon the bourgeois regime by means of suitable techniques. It will then institute the dictatorship of the proletariat which will be identified with that of the Party since, in the Marx-Leninist view and according to Marx himself, the Communists are the most advanced sector of the working-class world, the sector which *knows*. "The Communists", wrote Karl Marx in the *Communist Manifesto*, "have that advantage over the proletarian masses which is conferred by an understanding of the conditions, the progress and the general results of the proletarian movement."

This understanding of the conditions and of the progress of the proletarian movement, this *knowledge*, is provided for them by Karl Marx who gave them the method and the example of an economic and social analysis based on this method. The politics, sociology and world view of Marxism are therefore inseparable. Marxism is a total phenomenon. In actual fact, a dogmatic position has modified the conditions of this *knowledge* in the Marxist world. It is the leaders who know and who think for the masses, and the interests of the proletarian movement have become confused with those of a particular nation and, today, with those of a group of nations.

CHAPTER IV

COMMUNISM, THE FAMILY AND PRIVATE PROPERTY

When in the first chapter we pointed out that the Church in her condemnation of Communism tended to emphasize more and more the atheistic aspect of the latter, we underlined the fact that the condemnations issued in the name of the natural law, and directed against one or other of Communism's more characteristic ideas, were not thereby any the less forceful. These condemnations are directly aimed at the Communist concept of the nature of the family and of the right to property. It is therefore time that we examined them.

In estimating the difference between the Christian and Communist concepts, we shall not lose sight of the fact that the source of this difference lies not so much in the fact that Communism considers that society evolves, as in its relativist concept of human values and of law, whereas Christianity refers all values to an Absolute.

MARX-LENINISM AND THE FAMILY

At the beginning of his career, while he was still only engaged, Karl Marx dealt with the problem of marriage in three articles in the *Rheinische Zeitung* (August 25th, November 15th and December 13th, 1842). He wrote from the standpoint of the philosophy of law. In the first article he criticized a manifesto of the School of Legal History and declared himself in favour of monogamy. In the other two he criticized the Prussian draft bill on divorce. He attacked the idea of marriage as developed by Hegel who deduced from it that marriage is indissoluble. For Marx, marriage is not an idea but a social fact and "a divorce is no more than a statement that this marriage has ceased to be a marriage and its existence is no more than mere semblance and imposture".

In the *Economic and Philosophical Manuscripts of 1844*, treating of the relationship between private property and Communism and of the relationships between man and woman, Marx protested against "a gross and senseless form of Communism" inspired by Fourier's ideas and demanding that wives should be common property. On the contrary, he continued:

> The immediate and necessary relationship between one human being and another is the relationship between *man and woman*. In this *natural*, generic relationship, man's relation to nature is without more ado his relation to mankind, just as man's relation to mankind is without more ado his relationship with nature . . . that which makes him human. Hence this relationship shows forth in a visible way, makes outwardly obvious the extent to which for mankind the essence of man has become "nature", and the extent to which "nature" has become the essence of man. This is why, on the basis of this relation, we can estimate the degree of man's evolution.

Marx, therefore, after making the profound observation that the sexual relations of man and woman fully reveal the mutual relations of man with mankind and of man with nature, rejects the community of wives proper to primitive Communism.

Similarly, he rejects bourgeois marriage because it is "undoubtedly an exclusive form of private property" and private property has produced in man a sense of possession through which he suffers the loss of himself. It is a form of degradation, a loss of human status. So the bourgeois marriage is obviously dehumanizing and only the suppression of private property in all its forms completely frees from bondage all forms of ownership, all forms of man's sensitivity, since by it man will become genuinely human.

In the *Communist Manifesto*, Marx embarked on a very drastic criticism of the bourgeois family. He restated his previous argument in shorter and less philosophical terms. "What", he asked, "is the basis of the family of today, the bourgeois family? Capital, the private acquisition of wealth. The family exists in its complete form for the bourgeoisie alone, but it has as its corollary the total disappearance of the family among the proletarians, and public prostitution. The bourgeois family will of course disappear together with the corollary which is its complement. Both will vanish when capital disappears." Yet Marx did not go so far as to say what the relationships between man and woman would be under "absolute Communism". The question remains an open one.

In 1877, L. H. Morgan's book *Ancient Society* was published in London. It once more drew the attention of Marx and Engels to the problem of the family. On the authority of L. H. Morgan's work, Engels now wrote his *Origin of the Family, Private Property and the State*, in which he showed that the introduction of private property enslaved woman to man. Engels, who saw in monogamy the highest form of sexual relationships, considered that with the disappearance of prostitution after the socialist revolution, a genuine, fully developed monogamy inspired by love would be established. In point of fact, Engel's attitude remained a cautious one for he added: "What we may expect from the organization of sexual relationships, after the forthcoming clean sweep of capitalist production, is principally of a negative character and limited in the main to what will disappear."

What in his opinion will disappear from monogamy as practised in bourgeois society where it is dominated by the conditions induced by private property is, on the one hand, the preponderant rôle of the male sex and, on the other, the indissolubility of marriage.

Engels does not clearly state what will happen to the family after capitalist society is transformed into a socialist and then a Communist society in which "the free development of each will be the condition of the free development of all". In this, he is faithful to Marx who refused to offer recipes for the "cookhouses of the future". The new generations of men and women will decide, for they will know only "true love" and will be freed from the fear of the economic consequences of a possible desertion of the wife by the husband. "When these people come into existence, they will not care a damn what we now think they ought to do. They will form their own customs and a public opinion which will judge the individual's conduct. And that is all there is to it!"

The institution of the family, the law which gives it an objective foundation, are part of the superstructure of society and depend on economic structures and on nothing else. As Morgan wrote—and Engels adopts his point of view—"The family . . . must advance as society advances, and change as society changes." And Engels adds that if, one day, the monogamous family should not fulfil the demands of society, it is impossible to predict what type of family would take its place.

With this sort of beginning, free love is not far away. Love will depend entirely on a "mutual inclination" and if this disappears for one reason or another (genuinely or ousted by a new passion), separation, Engels concludes, will be a benefit for all and for society.

Engels's idealism opened the door to every kind of abuse. Lenin, who was more of a realist, reacted against it. He did not want young people to claim in the name of Marxism a right to uncontrolled sexual liberty, free from "all serious thought of love" and from "all notion of procreation" or asserting "the freedom to commit adultery".

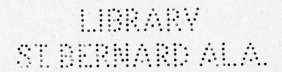

Lenin attacked both the bourgeois Malthusian theories and free love, that other form of bourgeois decadence. He wrote twice (January 17th and 24th, 1915) to Inès Armand who was preparing to defend free love in a pamphlet for working-class women. He tells her: "free love—this is what the bourgeois demands, not the proletarian". He contrasts with it "the objective logic of class relationships in the sphere of love" and invites her to contrast "base, filthy, loveless marriage" with the "love-marriage of the proletarian".

In 1920, he expressed similar views in his conversations with Clara Zetkin. He attacked the "theory of the glass of water" and the profligacy to which it gave rise among Soviet youth. "I consider that the celebrated theory of the glass of water[1] is un-Marxist and anti-social to boot. . . . True, a drink of water is a personal affair. But when it is a question of love, there are two interested parties and a third joins them, a new creature. It is at this point that the interests of society are involved and a duty towards the collectivity arises." Lenin then details a whole programme of manly education for youth and adds: "The Revolution demands the concentration and the tension of forces both in the masses and in isolated individuals."

In a survey written about the same time, Alexandra Kollontaï, who was considered to be the spokeswoman of the Bolshevist Communist Party in matters concerning women, stated:

> The family is ceasing to be a necessity for the members who compose it as well as for the State. . . . In the Communist society, all forms of housework will become unnecessary. They will be replaced by central kitchens, restaurants and wash-houses and special workshops for repairs to clothing. The

[1] The "theory of the glass of water" was that in Communist society the satisfaction of sexual desires, of love, would be as simple and unimportant as "drinking a glass of water". See Clara Zetkin, *Reminiscences of Lenin*, New York, International Publishers, 1934, p. 49.

working-class woman will certainly have no further cause to regret the disappearance of domestic chores. Society will have abolished the woman's domestic yoke only in order to give her a richer, fuller, happier and freer life. As for the children, they will be taken over and educated by the State. The workers' society needs new labour forces, it welcomes the coming into the world of each newborn child. Do not be anxious any longer about your child's future. It will be neither hungry nor cold, it will be neither unhappy nor abandoned to its fate as it would have been under the capitalist regime. . . . The Communist Fatherland will see that it is fed, reared and educated. But the Fatherland will take care not to tear it away from those parents who want to share in the child's education. Communist society will assume responsibility for children's education but it will leave the joys of parenthood to those who show themselves fit to understand and appreciate them. For the former type of family, which has had its day, there will be substituted the bond of affection and comradeship, the union of two equal members of the Communist society, both free, both independent, both workers.

After a preparatory period (1917–25) an attempt was made from 1926 to 1936 to impose Marxist ideas on the family with the adoption of the second *Marriage and Family Code*. Its net result was a signal failure on the social and economic plane as well as on that of morals. The 1926 Code introduced into Soviet legislation the *de facto* marriage and divorce by mutual consent. Legislation was moving further and further from the traditional idea of the family. But at the same time a certain number of social abuses of some importance resulted from this legislation—women with children in their care were deserted by their husbands, children were abandoned, there were refusals to pay alimony and juvenile crime increased.

At the instigation of the public authorities, a reaction set in after the partial success of the first Five-Year plan. In 1936 it led to measures which, though they did not restore the traditional concepts of marriage and the family, restricted the working of the 1926 Code and annulled in practice certain of its most harmful provisions.

After the immense slaughter of the second World War (1941–5) more radical measures became necessary. It was discovered that a stable family institution is essential if society is to develop. Temporary unions were discouraged by means of alimony regulations, *de facto* marriage and divorce by mutual consent were, for all practical purposes, abolished, grounds for divorce were restricted, the courts were instructed not to grant it except where no other solution was possible, and even then to attend to the welfare of the children and to keep in mind the social repercussions of divorce.

The Communist movement, particularly in the various European countries, adopted the new Soviet idea of marriage and the family. From 1935 onwards, emphasis was laid on the protection of the mother and child and after the second World War there was a demand for a family policy which would explicitly recognize the rights of mothers.

In fact, as far as the family in the Soviet Union is concerned, Marxist ideology and legislation have had to take into account the permanent factors in human nature, the more or less vigorous protests of the human conscience and the pressure of social realities.

But the fundamental ideas of Marxism in regard to marriage and the family continue to be preached or defended in the U.S.S.R. From time to time press articles appear and their publication leads one to suppose that the stage inaugurated by the 1944 decrees may well be only a passing phase and not a return to a natural order.

Further, certain aspects of the ideology in relation to the family have remained unchanged from the days of Marx and Engels down to those of the present Soviet Union. The Soviets hold with Engels that "the care of children and their education become the business of the community. Society takes equal care of all children whether legitimate or natural."

After the disastrous adventure described above, the Soviets, like Engels, admit that "as sexual love is of its nature exclusive, marriage is based on monogamy". The stale odours of the gross Communism stigmatized by Marx, and of the Saint-Simonism and Fouriérism present at the beginning of the 1917 Revolution, have now been dispelled by the 1944 legislation.

There is a closer continuity than one might think at first sight between Engels who rejected the bourgeois idea of marriage which is a "contract, a legal affair" and the Soviet idea which restored the contract as the basis of marriage. "Socialist family relationships are very clearly characterized by a harmonious synthesis of the principle of the free expression of the will and the regulating activity of the State as source of liberty and discipline", writes the Soviet jurist G. M. Sverdlov. And it was Engels who wrote: "Complete freedom to marry cannot be generally achieved until the suppression of capitalist production, and the property provisions it has created, has done away with all secondary economic considerations. . . . Then there will be no longer any incentive to marry other than mutual inclination." This is the Soviet assertion of the principle of the free expression of the will. As for the regulating activity of the State, in the Soviet view it does not contradict the principle of the free expression of the will, since there is so close a connection established by the Soviets between the State and the proletarian conscience. It helps free will to find its direction and to discipline itself. So much so that G. M. Sverdlov is consistent with himself and with Soviet practice when he repeats and applies to the family the remark made by Stalin to H. G. Wells in 1934: "Socialism does not reject, it reconciles individual interests with those of society", and when he considers that the family is "one of the social forms which satisfy at one and the same time the interests of the individual and of society".

But it is equally obvious that in fact the pattern of family relationships depends to a very great extent on the State which becomes the controlling force in the evolution of the concept and the reality of marriage to the extent that public opinion does not intervene in order to put a check on the intentions of the governing authorities. This was the case at the beginning of the Revolution when the marriage legislation was promulgated; it is the case also (in the opposite sense, it is true) as regards the application of the 1944 legislation, although the latter is closer to the requirements of the natural law. The "complete freedom to marry" foreseen by Engels, depends, under a socialist regime, upon what the State understands by the harmonization of individual interests and those of society. Once this has been said, it must be admitted that there is some progress at present in comparison with the state of affairs during the first twenty years of the Revolution, in so far as recent legislation, the practice of the courts and the training of the young to respect the family have begun to put matters right where the latter is concerned. But this progress cannot be ascribed to the dialectical development of Marx-Leninist ideology. It is the outcome of the pressure of social facts and of a more accurate evaluation by the Soviet authorities of the means to be adopted in pursuit of their aim, that is, the creation of "the total man", that "most valuable form of capital".

This is not the place to enlarge upon the Christian concept of the family, which has nothing in common with the "bourgeois" concept criticized by Marx and by subsequent Marxism. But what must be noted is that the idea of the family according to Marxism is directly linked with the idea of man as a worker. This is the starting point of Marx's analyses as early as in his *German Ideology*. In the same passage where he noted that the primordial historical fact is man's production of the means by which his needs are satisfied—his need to eat, to drink, to have a place to live in, to clothe himself and the rest—Karl Marx continues:

The third point which arises at once in the process of historical development is the fact that men, who renew their own lives every day, begin by giving birth to others, begin by reproducing themselves. Hence the relations between man and woman, parents and children, hence the *family*. The family, which in the beginning is the only social relationship, becomes, once social life has developed, something subordinate and must then be treated and developed according to the existing empirical data.

Thus the family is thought of merely in relation to economic life and is an institution subordinated to the economic relationships which are established among men. This is to deny that specific character of the family in human society which is asserted by the whole body of Christian thought.

Subjected to an evolutionary process whose term is only vaguely defined as the freedom of love, the family falls under the domination of the socialist State which then has complete power to modify according to circumstances not only the family's structure but also its nature. And nothing justifies us in claiming that, once the indissolubility of man's relationship with woman within the family has been broken, a revival of this indissolubility is anything more than a passing phase in the journey towards this vaguely defined goal. By considering the family primarily from the angle of biological and economic life, Marxism rejects the distinction between the nature of the marriage bond whose indissolubility derives from the nature of marriage, and the freedom to enter into marriage which Christianity has always taken care to safeguard to the full, and which derives from the freedom of the human will.

By asserting that the relations between husband and wife are founded on their recognition of a reciprocal priority of each over the other which involves a respect for the different and, at the same time, complementary vocation of the partner, Christianity safeguards, deepens, disciplines and spiritualizes love through personal respect, even if mistakes and human failures, which are always possible, should occur. In actual practice, such an achievement is denied to "freedom of love" extolled by Marxism as the ultimate goal, subordinated as it is to circumstances and the caprices of passion.

MARXISM AND PROPERTY

Marx's position in regard to property is well known. "What characterizes Communism", he wrote in 1848 in the *Communist Manifesto*, "is not that it abolishes property as such, but that it abolishes bourgeois property.... In this sense Communists are entitled to sum up their theory in the formula, the abolition of private property." This is the formula in common use. It corresponds to that launched by Brissot and de Warville in 1782 and adopted by Proudhon in 1840, "Property is theft".

Marx's position cannot be reduced to the single formula— the abolition of the system of private property. As editor of the *Rheinische Zeitung* from 1842 onwards, Karl Marx was faced with the problem of property when he had to criticize the debates in the Rhineland Diet on the bill aimed at preventing thefts of wood. "This law represented one of the phases of the struggle waged by capitalism against the last vestiges of the common ownership of land." He had occasion to reflect upon it again when he undertook a critical study of Hegel's *Philosophy of Right* during the year 1843. The problem then was to test the value of Hegel's conclusions in favour of "entailed property" which guaranteed to the Prussian aristocracy the permanent possession of their landed property.

Beginning with a critical analysis of previous and contemporary forms of property (or, more accurately, the system of ownership of goods and chattels) and of their origin, Karl Marx somewhat later established a connection between these forms of appropriation (varying according to the period and to the type of society) and the economic and social systems. Beneath the institutions, economic categories and the law's "juridical illusion" he sought to reveal the reality of the human relationships which they overlay. Hence, in Marx's concept we find a complex reality, as is evidenced by his remark to Paul Annenkov concerning Proudhon: "Property forms the final category in Proudhon's system. In the real world, on the other hand, the division of labour and the rest of M. Proudhon's categories are social relationships and together they form what is now called property."

Summing up in 1859 the tasks of his first fifteen years of political life, Karl Marx wrote: "At a certain stage of their development the productive forces of society find themselves at variance with the existing production relationships or with what is merely their juridical expression, namely, the property relationships within which they have hitherto operated." Already in a passage of the *Communist Manifesto*, where he made a résumé of the analyses in his *German Ideology*, he had written of the evolution from feudal to bourgeois society: "We have seen these modes of production and these means of communication (which made possible the formation of the bourgeoisie) become, at a certain stage of their growth, compatible with the conditions of production and exchange, agriculture and manufacture of feudal society, in a word, with the feudal system of property." Similarly, of the social conflicts at the beginning of the century in England and France, he wrote: "For the past few decades, the history of industry and commerce is nothing other than the history of the revolt of modern productive forces against modern production relationships, against the system of property upon which depends the very existence and sovereignty of the bourgeoisie."

If the whole complex of property relationships is the juridical expression of the existing production relationships, it is because, in Marx's view, "the primal historical fact is the production of the means of satisfying these needs (that is, the need of man to drink, eat, find a place to live in, clothe himself), the production of material life itself", and it leads men to take possession of nature directly or indirectly to an ever increasing extent. In the unpublished Introduction to the *Critique of Political Economy* he wrote: "All production is an appropriation of nature by the individual within and by means of a given form of society. In this sense it is tautologous to say that property (appropriation) is a condition of production. . . . To say that there can be no possibility of production, and so of any society, without the existence of property, is a tautology. An appropriation which appropriates nothing is a *contradictio in subjecto*."

At the same time in the *Economic Manuscripts of 1857–8*, published only very recently, and which were preparatory to the composition of his *Contribution to a Critique of Political Economy* and to a lesser extent of *Capital*, Marx wrote: "Property is a specific relationship (of man) with the conditions of production in so far as they are his own . . . (it) only exists by reason of production. Effective appropriation is realized in the first place not through an intellectual relationship but through a real, effective relationship with these conditions of production and their effective use as a condition of (man's) subjective activity."

But with the development of the division of labour within successive societies and that of the productive forces, the basis of the relationship changes to such an extent that it becomes its own exact opposite. According to Marx: "In the beginning the right to property was based on personal work" and in the Middle Ages "each man's individual work was still his own sole property". In our times, on the contrary, we find ourselves facing "a total rupture between property and work". "Property is revealed in the capitalist as the right of appropriating to himself without payment the work of others or the product of this work, and in the worker as a denial of the possibility of appropriating to himself what he himself produces."

According to Marx, this is the result of the development of the capitalist regime in which an apparent exchange of equivalents in the labour market really serves as a cloak for an exchange of non-equivalents. Marx studies this at great length in the first book of *Capital*. It is at the root of surplus-value and of the process by which capital accumulates. In the end the worker is separated from the product of his work. In so far as the economic system treats the end product of work as an article of merchandise, the worker is cut off from the product of his work, as Marx explained at length in one of the *Economical and Philosophical Manuscripts of 1844*. "By its inevitable and inherent dialectic, the law of appropriation or the law of private property, based on the production and marketing of goods, is transformed into its precise opposite." There is a radical separation of property from work. "Just as the production of goods at a certain stage in its development necessarily becomes capitalist production ... so the laws of property regulating the production of goods are equally bound to change into laws of capitalist appropriation." Under the capitalist regime the wage-earner is despoiled of the fruits of his creative activity which gave him human status, and this by the very process of economic development.

But history cannot remain at this stage. The existing property relationships become an impediment to the development of the forces of production and to that of man's mastery over nature. "The productive forces which develop within bourgeois society create at the same time the material conditions necessary to remove this opposition" between production and property relationships. Further, with the solution of this conflict "the pre-history of human society comes to an end". For a class develops "from which springs an awareness of the need for a radical revolution".

Continuing the formulation of the dialectic of pre-capitalist forms of property, which Marx had undertaken in *German Ideology* and the *Economic Manuscripts of 1857–8*, Engels sums up the process of their development in his *Anti-Dühring*:

> All civilized peoples begin with common ownership of land.
> Among all peoples who pass beyond a certain primitive stage
> this common property becomes an obstacle to production as
> agriculture evolves. It is abolished, repudiated, transformed
> into private property after more or less lengthy intermediate
> stages. But at a higher level of agricultural development, itself
> the result of private ownership of the land, the converse is true
> and private ownership becomes an obstacle to production, as
> it is today in the case of both small and large landed property.
> There inevitably arises a demand that it too be repudiated and
> changed back into common property. But this demand does
> not mean the restoration of the ancient, primitive, common
> ownership, but the establishment of a far higher and more
> developed form of collective ownership which, far from be-
> coming a barrier to production, will for the first time un-
> shackle it and allow it the full use of chemical discoveries and
> modern mechanical inventions.

Although Marx considers that the Communist programme
can be summed up in the formula "the abolition of private
property", it is not any sort of private property that is meant.
"There is no need for us to abolish the property of the small
shopkeeper or peasant which existed before the advent of
bourgeois ownership. The development of industry has
already been abolishing it and goes on abolishing it day by
day." It is modern "bourgeois private property (which) is the
ultimate and final expression of a state of things in which
production and the appropriation of its products are conditioned by a struggle between the classes, by an exploitation
of man by man". It is capitalist property which is to be
abolished. And the reason for this is that "to be a capitalist
is not only to have a certain personal position, it is to occupy
a social position in the production process". If "capital is not
a power attached to an individual person but a power inherent
in society", we must give it back its first purpose and make of
it "a collective property, belonging to all members of society".

By so doing, we shall not "transform personal property into collective property, what will be changed is the social character of ownership".

In Marx's view, every form of private ownership of the means of production, whether on a large or small scale, should be abolished. The small property of the peasant or the artisan has been abolished to all intents and purposes by capitalism, it no longer enters into the picture. At the time when he was writing, Marx considered that it was sufficient to abolish capitalist private ownership of the means of production. He was deeply suspicious of "cooperative production societies subsidized by the capitalist State. They are only of value in so far as they are independent institutions in the hands of the workers." He had nothing to say about them under a socialist regime. He made no mention of the private ownership of consumer goods except in his *Critique of the Gotha Programme* in which he stated that such goods will be handed over to the workers in return for exchange bonds by distribution agencies which will draw from the "social stocks" of the socialist State during the first phase of Communism. In any case Marx has little to say about the methods of sharing out the consumer goods that are produced. For him these methods vary with those of production and in line with the evolution of the latter. The upshot of this analysis makes it quite clear that Marx's approach to the problem of property is different from that of the jurists. This is because for him "bourgeois ownership, apart from these (social) relationships, is no more than a metaphysical and juridical illusion". The law of property as developed in the *Treatises on Civil Law* belongs to the world of "prevailing ideas" corresponding to a given economic reality, and by means of which "the class, having at its disposal the means of production", imposes its domination, even in the sphere of thought, thanks to its "active ideologies".

For Marx there is no property nor any right to property in an absolute sense. There are forms of property, of appropriation, and of systems of ownership of goods, all of which are themselves contingent.

Marx's genetic and critical studies of the various forms of appropriation lead to the following results:

They emphasize, on the one hand, the link existing between property relationships, which are the juridical expression of the social production relationships within a given society, and the appropriation by man of the products of the work done.

On the other, they show that beneath the apparent stability (or unity) throughout time of the system of ownership of goods, the distribution of goods varies continually as the result of the evolution of production methods (organization and division of labour, etc). This evolution fundamentally alters the whole meaning of the word "distribution".

Unlike the jurists who conduct a formal analysis, Karl Marx studied the place of ownership in the liberal economic and political system of his times. Starting from the notion that man is a being who produces his own life and himself, he had come to the conclusion that through this self-production man entered into possession of his own being. And it is this meaning of property—that fundamental phenomenon which dominates the whole history of humanity—which he expounds in the *Economic and Philosophical Manuscripts of 1844* and in *German Ideology*. Property, by becoming private in the capitalist system, has become a source of exploitation, and appropriation is effected against man's interests. It is by appropriating the product of his activity that man should enter into possession of himself. Instead of this man has suffered the loss of himself.

Property and political power are closely connected in the thought of Marx and Engels. The latter thought he had found in the idea of private property the principle which allowed the State to emerge. The Soviets—those who, with Lenin, came before the 1917 Revolution, and also their continuators—inherited these fundamental ideas. They established a necessary link between political authority and economic power conferred by the ownership of the means of production. Even the opponents of the regime were in agreement upon this point, Trotsky for instance in his *The Revolution Betrayed* (1936). "In the eyes of the Soviet intellectual, property is seen to be fundamental in the acquisition and preservation of power." This is enough to make us understand the capital importance of the problems relating to the right to property and to the system of distribution of goods in the Soviet and every Communist regime of Marxist type.

The opposition of Marx and of later Marxism to private property has therefore a twofold basis. On the one hand, it derives from the concept of man the worker. In 1844 Marx wrote: "Private property as activity for its own sake, as subject, as *person*, is work." Once the system of ownership in practice denies this assertion and, by the same token, prevents man from realizing his own being and leaves him despoiled and naked, then the private appropriation of any kind of goods must be opposed. On the other hand, the historical analysis undertaken by Marx led him to think that the ownership of producer goods, the source of economic power over men, puts political power (the power that enables man to dominate over man by means of the State) into the hands of private owners. "At the historical base of every social system", wrote a Soviet author a few years ago, "we find a specific historical form of ownership. Hence the question of property has always been one of the most topical in the history of human society."

Marxism therefore proposes to suppress both the right and the system of private ownership of goods, and this both because of the abuses to which a system of private ownership of goods gives rise, and also as a consequence of its view that work is the only source of ownership.

The Christian position is very different. Christianity does not fail to recognize the abuses resulting from certain forms of private ownership of goods. It does not condone these abuses. But it maintains the right of private ownership, by opposing the pure and simple identification of the implications of this right with any given existing system of private ownership.

In 1848, when Marx published the *Communist Manifesto*, Mgr Ketteler, bishop of Mainz, while protesting against the formula of Proudhon "Property is theft", declared publicly: "The truth contained in this formula must be destroyed if the formula is one day to become a complete lie. As long as it contains a grain of truth, it is powerful enough to turn the whole world order upside down. As deep calls unto deep, so one crime against nature leads to another. The false theory of property is the outcome of a false right to property."[1]

Private appropriation as understood by Christian thought cannot indeed be confused with an uncontrolled, perpetual possession (that cannot be reviewed except in a few cases provided for by the civil law) of all the goods which an individual may acquire in an economic system, where the fertility of money is one of the essential laws and the exploitation of man is more than a gratuitous hypothesis.

Pius XI in *Quadragesimo Anno* (1931) vigorously and shrewdly reproached the capitalist system for leading a few men to take possession of both economic and political power, and in the process, for treating man, like the Marxists, as "the most valuable form of capital". He wrote:

> In the first place, then, it is patent that in our days not wealth alone is accumulated but immense power and despotic economic domination are concentrated in the hands of a few, who for the most part are not the owners, but only the trustees and directors of invested funds which they administer at their own good pleasure.
>
> This domination is most powerfully exercised by those who,

[1] Quoted by Rutten, *La Doctrine sociale de l'Eglise*, Ed. du Cerf, pp. 101–2.

because they hold and control money, also govern credit and determine its allotment. . . .

This accumulation of power has, in its turn, led to a three-fold struggle. First, there is the struggle for economic supremacy itself; then the fierce battle to acquire control of the State, so that its resources and authority may be abused in economic struggles; finally the clash between States themselves.[2]

The forms of ownership and capital are not immutable as Pius XI reminded us in a speech to the Committee of Italian Catholic Action (May 16th, 1926);

There is an uncertainty from which nothing can escape, for the essence of created things resides in it. These are not in themselves their own *raison d'être*. Hence it comes about that even for things of the greatest importance, for those that are most intimately connected with the very substance of certain institutions, uncertainty is possible and sometimes inevitable. In fact, it is even normal. . . . It is precisely in those social factors which are least liable to change, such as property, capital, work, that a host of alterations is not only possible in the formation of the pattern of their relationships, but a real and accomplished fact. We have only to look at history.

Pius XI repeated these assertions in *Quadragesimo Anno* (1931) and applied them to property in particular. Pius XII did likewise and referred to this Encyclical in his speech of June 1st, 1941, commemorating the fiftieth anniversary of Leo XIII's Encyclical *Rerum Novarum*.

In dealing with the problem of private property Christianity defends an *idea* and a *right* to private ownership which have little to do with the the *forms* which this institution may have taken within various systems, the liberal capitalist system in particular. On September 1st, 1944, Pius XII drew attention to two important points:

[2] Pius XI Encycl. *Quadragesimo Anno*, translation from revised edition issued by the Catholic Social Guild, sections 105–8.

1. The Christian conscience cannot recognize a social order as just which denies in principle or in practice makes impossible or of no avail the natural right to the ownership of both consumer and producer goods.

2. But neither can it compromise with those systems which, while recognizing the right of private property, do so in accordance with an absolutely false concept, and are thus opposed to a genuine and healthy social order. That is why, for example, in cases where "capitalism" is based on these erroneous conceptions and arrogates to itself an unlimited right over ownership with no reference whatsoever to the common good, the Church has always condemned it as contrary to the natural law.

As Pius XII pointed out in his speech of June 1st, 1941, Christianity asserts at one and the same time the right to the collective use of material goods and the right of private ownership.

Every man as a living creature endowed with reason, receives *de facto* from nature the fundamental right to use the material goods of the earth, although it is left to the human will and to the juridical systems of the nations to regulate in greater detail the practical exercise of this right. Such an individual right cannot be in any way suppressed, not even by other certain and recognized rights over material goods. Undoubtedly, the natural order which comes from God also requires that there should be private ownership and freedom for reciprocal trading in goods by means of exchange and donations. It requires too that public authority should have a regulating function in regard to each of these institutions. All this, nevertheless, remains subordinated to the natural end of material goods, and cannot be made independent of the primary and fundamental right which concedes their use to all men. Rather should it serve to make possible the exercise of this right in conformity with this end.

This is equivalent to stating that, in proportion to his necessities, every man has the right to obtain what he needs, and that only a law which ensures that material goods are respected and their common purpose achieved, a law which also makes it possible for man to have personal access to these goods *quantum ad potestatem utendi ipsius*,[3] will be consistent with Christianity.

Private property then is recognized as a power which every man has over a specific portion of the earth's wealth—the power to manage it, to dispose of it and to assign it freely, but always in subordination to the common good of all men. Hence this power involves great personal responsibilities, which positive law does not allow men to elude.

In 1944, Pius XII repeated an assertion of Leo XIII: "Every normal economic and social order must be based on the solid foundation of the right to personal property", understood in this sense, so that each man and his family may be assured of "a sphere of liberty with justice, not only in economic, but also in political, cultural and religious affairs". In other words, as we might comment, "this establishment round the human person, of *a zone of security*, a kind of economic bulwark, seems to us a new function—hitherto little developed yet of capital importance—of a certain form of personal ownership in the presence of an economy whose very mechanism urges it towards a partial and perhaps progressive collectivization".[4]

While Karl Marx and Marxism see in the system of private property under a capitalist regime one of the causes of the exploitation of man and of the loss of human freedom, Christianity sees in the assertion of the right to property and in the institution of a system of private ownership (when effectively contained within limits fixed by the fundamental right of man to the common use of the goods of the earth) the source of true liberty for men in their life upon this earth.

It is because Christianity considers that the family and private property, understood in the sense defined above, are

[3] St Thomas Aquinas, *Summa Theologica*, IIa–IIae, Qu. 67, art. 1.
[4] E. Mounier, *Liberté sous conditions*, Ed. du Seuil, Paris, p. 160.

natural data, that it continues to insist on them and to defend them against Communism which denies them or considers them to be temporary institutions linked to one period of the economic development of mankind. "According to the doctrine of *Rerum Novarum*", Pius XII declared in 1941:

> Nature herself has closely linked private ownership with the existence of human society and its true civilization, but also, in an eminent degree, with the existence and development of the family. Is it not private ownership which is to ensure for the father of a family that healthy freedom that he needs if he is to be able to fulfil the duties assigned to him by the Creator, for the physical, spiritual and religious well-being of the family?

Consequently, the Christian cannot be content to agree passively with any and every view of the right to ownership, with any and every system of private property. By concerted action he must work and struggle for the establishment of a regime of private ownership in keeping with the requirements revealed to him by Christianity.

CHAPTER V

CATHOLICISM AND
COMMUNISM

At the end of the brief analysis which we have just made, Marx-Leninism (or Communism) stands forth as a *total phenomenon*. It is this aspect of *totality* which is its characteristic note, so that, though it is possible to isolate one or other of its elements, one or other of its analyses, it is only within this totality that they have meaning, and it is this totality which gives them this meaning.

Hence it is not enough for a philosopher or a scientist to deal with man as a social being, with the forms of human exploitation in the modern world or with evolution as an explanatory hypothesis, in order to be a Marxist or for his thought to derive from Marxism.

Conversely, it would not be possible to christianize Marxism by "baptizing" one or other of the parts of its system or by revising it in one or other of its aspects. Marxism could not be christianized except as a whole, and there is no question of that. Moreover Engels, as early as in 1843, had given a warning that there could be no possibility of envisaging a Christian Communism that would be Communism in the sense in which Karl Marx and he himself understood it.

THE INQUIRY INTO THE UNIVERSE OF MANKIND

Marxism aims to be at one and the same time a *full inquiry* into, and a *full explanation* of, the visible world of man. "It is a critique of daily life", wrote Henri Lefebvre. It denounces the exploitation of man within the various structures of present-day social life—religion, morality, philosophy, law, the State, economy. In its analysis of these, we are carried forward from one form of exploitation to another, until the basic form is reached, that is, economic exploitation. There is therefore an intrinsic link between the atheist project and the analyses and economic ideas of Marx and his successors.

The theory of value elaborated by Marx, whose starting point was in the ideas of the "classical" English economists Adam Smith and Ricardo, is as closely linked as the rejection of God and the profession of a practical atheism to Marx's central concept of man as a worker and *nothing but* a worker in the world of nature with which he grapples. The critique of daily life worked out by Marx and accepted by all his successors, whoever they may be, leads to the conclusion that man is sufficient unto himself, that his roots are in a history which is only that of his own production, and that there are no values other than those created by his work.

It is no doubt possible to point out that the way in which some Christians expounded Christianity favoured the adoption by Marx of this radically atheist concept of man. It can indeed be shown that the criticism of creation which he brings forward in the *Economic and Philosophical Manuscripts of 1844* does not really strike at the Christian doctrine of creation (which cannot strictly be identified with a process of making). Marx may have been unfavourably impressed by the presentation of the classical arguments for the existence of God which he had before him. That this may have been so is suggested by a reading of the rough preparatory drafts of his thesis on the *Difference between the Philosophies of Nature of Democritus and Epicurus*. But there is nothing to show that this presentation was in fact the correct one. His criticisms in this field also are therefore wide of the mark.

It is no doubt equally possible to point out that, like many of his contemporaries—Proudhon for instance—he was shocked by the manner in which Christianity, the established authorities and private interests were sometimes associated. But to conclude from this that, had things been otherwise, Marx would have evolved a doctrine acceptable to Christianity is a totally different matter. It is to forget that Marx also rejected the idea of the religion of Christian brotherhood as formulated by Lamennais and which so deeply impressed a certain number of French and German Socialists and Communists in the eighteen forties.

It is to forget that, contrary to what some assert, there are a certain number of presuppositions accepted uncritically at the starting point of Karl Marx's thought and action.

At the outset there is the same assumption as in the Hegelian system, namely that religion is a "moment" in the dialectic which leads consciousness to absolute Knowledge, so that religion is an element of philosophy. This idea is taken up again by all subsequent Marxism, in particular by Soviet and French Communism.

It will then be easy to see religion as an element in the superstructure *fabricated* by man the worker and to reduce it in all its forms to the level of a sociological phenomenon, as do Marx and Marxism at the outset of their thought. They also accept at the outset Feuerbach's conception of the nature of religion. "For Feuerbach, God is only the sum total of the attributes which make up the greatness of man", notes Fr H. de Lubac.[1] Feuerbach himself wrote: "It is man's own essence which is the supreme being. . . . If the divinity of nature is the basis of all religion, Christianity included, the divinity of man is its ultimate aim. . . . The turning point of history will be the moment when man becomes aware that his only god is man himself, *homo homini Deus*."

As Engels noted as early as 1844, Marx followed the

[1]H. de Lubac, *The Drama of Atheistic Humanism*, London and New York, Sheed and Ward.

French and English materialist philosophers of the eighteenth century in accepting a philosophy of nature as a self-enclosed system. This philosophy is nevertheless dialectical, as Engels himself tried to prove at the end of his life. This teaching was not lost upon the Soviet Marxists who rediscovered it during the nineteen twenties.

All these scattered ingredients gathered and welded together by the central Hegelian idea of man as creative activity (but creative activity transferred to the plane of daily life), make religion also a *product*—and nothing more—of the activity of man the maker, but man despoiled, lost, exploited through the conditions in which he lives. They also make Marx's radical, practical atheism the substructure, the basis of all Marxism.

There is no need to insist again that such a conception is in every way incompatible with the Christian idea of religion or with Christianity in the concrete. For more than twenty years now this incompatibility has been emphasized. Fr Rideau has written:

> Although it may be admitted that social conditions have had a contaminating effect upon certain religious organizations, although again religious life may have its own deviations which are a danger for the human conscience, yet it cannot be denied that there exists an absolutely disinterested and eminently spiritual movement which has produced the finest examples of humanity, personalities abounding in qualities, enjoying a maximum of freedom and of development, and of all men most to be envied. Among them, besides the contemplatives of India and the prophets of Israel, is the unnumbered host of the Christian saints, Christ above all, unique and, humanly speaking, extraordinary, but with a doctrine which derives first and foremost from his *religion*, from his experience of the holiness of God. His existence and his life would be sufficient to justify the idea of the possibility of a relation with a Being in whom human consciousness transcends itself and discovers itself anew. We need only re-read the Gospels, Pascal's

Pensées, the third chapter of Bergson's *Deux Sources* [*Two Sources of Morality and Religion*], documents which on various counts are incomparable and of the highest importance. Christ at least is beyond criticism and although *he too* was subjected to certain sociological conditions, he rose above them by inaugurating that absolutely pure and open form of religion which is the Act of Love of a God who is conceived as Love in person, and he claimed the tribute of this love for the Man in whom he became incarnate. In him alone man's existence became one with his essence, in him the community of mankind became a virtual reality. And this act of Love by which man, while keeping his natural and biological energies, yet transcends himself through the call to a total giving and a life of absolute service to Love, is the sole fundamental fact of Christianity. The rest is an incidental superstructure.

It would be easy to show that every dogma and every form of religious life flows from this essential source. Born of the will of Christ, still more called forth by an ontological necessity, the Catholic Church has only one mission—to bring to the historical process this message in its essential simplicity and to re-present the mystery of Christ dying and rising again for love of man. She must therefore put on, in forms that are likewise contingent, the outward fashion of the Man-God, his visible, bodily appearance. Like her Founder and Master, she is the spiritual link between man and God and at the same time between man and man; she is the source of all community. Whether she has done her task well or ill, she is of the highest importance for mankind. Moreover, she herself and Christ are but answers to a fundamental and eternal longing of the human heart.

Man is in anguish, as both Existentialism and Communism recognize, because of his situation in which at various levels existence and essence are kept tragically apart, and he *desires* to be at one with himself, to become fully what he ideally is, to solve the mystery of his being, which for him is infinite suffering. And this dislocation, which is revealed in the inner conflict between what he is and what he wants to be, is carried over with equally tragic results into the social divisions, especially that of the classes. Man is his own enemy, man is the enemy of other men. A wound, which alas! he has willed and which is his sin, prevents him from reaching the good even while he longs for it. The weight of his egoism keeps him engulfed and imprisoned in matter. The Christian religion in its essence is simply the answer to the powerless desire of man's conscience. She asks him to accept her mediation so that he may find again his own personal and social essence, so that his own broken unity and that of society may be restored.

This mediation had itself to be personal and free, it had to be a Person and a free Person, for that which has no name is but an ineffectual speculative abstraction, a sterile idea. This mediation had to be transcendent if man were not to lay hold of it with a gesture of pride which would have increased his sinfulness. It had also to be immanent so that it should not be in him as an alien force and so unacceptable to him as a free creature. Finally, this mediation had to be both human and absolute, to unite in itself both Man and God.

All these requirements are realized in Christ, presented and represented by the Church in the mystery of his Body, made actual beneath the life-giving symbol of the Bread of Love and Communion. Henceforth it is impossible to be completely and concretely a man without going to the furthest limits of man's longing to make himself, and all humanity with him, divine. But there is a condition: man must personally accept the personal message and the personal presence in the historical process, of the Mediator of Love. Man can only be cured of the division within himself, can only transcend himself in the act of the absolute love of God and his brethren, even at the risk of his own life. But if this act of love is not to be a mere fiction or an act of pride, it must be made with the help, wholly interior though it may be, of him who is Love. Man only enters into his vocation and his essence by going to the furthest limits of his being and offering himself wholly and entirely in the sacrifice of Love.[2]

[2] E. Rideau, *Séduction communiste et réflexion chrétienne*, La Proue, Spès, Paris, 1947, pp. 223–7.

The radical opposition between Communism and Christianity which we have just underlined has its origin in the Marxist conception of man the worker, who is defined by the fact of being a worker, constructing his own self, autonomous, free from all relationship with God, in his daily conflict with nature. Not that Christianity rejects the idea of man transforming nature and humanizing it through his work. On the contrary, it is Christianity which, in defiance of the pagan ideas of work in the ancient world, revealed to man all its meaning and grandeur. So much so that, when this grandeur and this significance of human work are flouted by a civilization and an economic regime of whatever kind, it is the whole Christ who is attacked in every one of those who are the victims of the system. Even if it is not explicitly recognized, even if to some people it may seem corrupted, it is Christ's own protest which is at the heart of the protest of this system's victims. No man can serve two masters, God and Money—or God and Power.

By laying too great stress on a partial truth—man's physical incorporation into nature, which makes of him a creature who produces in order to satisfy his needs—Marxism eventually forces him into an inhuman universe. Physiological needs are not the only factor in history. "The dynamism of human *needs* has always a higher aim than their material satisfaction and never rests content with the possession of any specific object, for in the urges of animal nature there lies an infinite desire" (E. Rideau). The economic factor does not comprise the whole of "social" man nor is it the whole of human history.

By taking as its starting point the theory that man can be explained by his needs, and the fact that he is a being who works, the Marxist critique of the capitalist system achieves its aim—to show that capitalism is a temporary stage in human development—only by relying on an unscientific oversimplification.

Even though it happens to illuminate certain aspects of

man's condition under a capitalist regime that may justly be criticized, particularly in the case of the proletarian, its critique and the explanation it gives of the formation and evolution of the capitalist system are inaccurate or insufficient or else at variance with the part which, in the course of the explanation, it claims has been played by one factor or another. Passing in *Capital* from ethical considerations (often to the point in his earliest writings) to economic explanations, Karl Marx used concepts whose lack of complete definition hid from him a whole section of the reality which he was analysing.

Thus he evolved the theory of work as value—the corner-stone of the whole of *Capital*—and made it the basis of his critical analysis of the "classical" economic theories and of the capitalist system because he considered man to be essentially nothing more than a worker, an activity which creates goods and values. This is evident from an examination of his notes and from a comparison between different passages in the *Economic Manuscripts of 1844*, in which he analyses the essence of private property, exchange and their relationship. The exclusion of the other elements common to the products of human activity which he makes at the beginning of *Capital*, is only the transference of his fundamental concept to the economic field. Marx's theory of work as value is directly linked with this reduction of man to the sole status of a creative activity autonomous in the world of nature.

Once the theory of work as value and its application to the commodity "work"—economists object to both—are accepted, it is then easy to show that the system only develops by exploiting the proletarian from whom the capitalist during the production process extorts what becomes the surplus-value. This dispenses Marx from asking himself whether there are not other sources of surplus-values, such as technical progress and innovations, in a system that is never in equi-librium. We have noted in passing the same signs of uncertainty and the same deficiencies in scientific analysis in his study of the class structure of society. There is no need to go over the ground again.

Marx's critique and explanation of the capitalist system, even if they are sometimes seen to contain partially valid intuitions, owe their well-known but only apparent exactitude to rough guesses and over-simplified identifications that are out of place in a work claiming to be a scientific critique.

In short, the Marxist analysis of the world of man rests on a philosophical *a priori*, namely that man is defined above all by his work, and history by the creation of the instruments of work.

THE MARXIST PHILOSOPHY OF HISTORY AND ITS HOPES FOR THE FUTURE

Communism claims to do more than provide man with a critique of daily life and an explanation of the world; it offers itself as a hope for the future, as both a philosophy of freedom and a philosophy of history. And for Marxism, these are *practical* philosophies. As we have seen, Marxism so offers itself when it proposes to free man from various forms of exploitation, to lead him from the last stage of his "pre-history" to real history which marks the end of the conflict between man and nature and between man and man. In a word, it claims to introduce him to the reign of freedom, according to the phrase used by Karl Marx in the last book of *Capital*.

Marxism was a philosophy of history as early as in the opening passages of the *Communist Manifesto* where Marx asserts: "The whole history of human society hitherto is the history of class struggles", and where in a brief résumé he shows that history develops in the open or hidden struggle between free men and slaves in oriental society, between patricians and plebeians in Roman society, between barons and serfs during the feudal period, between master craftsmen and journeymen in the modern world and, finally, continues today between the capitalist bourgeoisie and the proletariat.

Here, he is only summarizing his long previous studies, *German Ideology* in particular. He had already had a fore-runner of genius in the person of Saint-Simon.

In his *Le Système Industriel* (1821-2) and in the *Catéchisme des Industriels* (1823-4), Saint-Simon considered that modern society is made up of two different social systems. In the first, whose foundations were laid in the Middle Ages before the eleventh century, "all the economic life of society depended on the lords and all its intellectual life upon the priests". No sooner was it instituted than it began to decay. The second slowly began to arise as soon as industrial and scientific forces took shape, developed and freed man from the shackles that impeded the exercise of his powers. It started in the movement for the emancipation of the communes in the twelfth century. But it is only from the sixteenth century onwards that the conflict between the two societies came to the full light of day and became increasingly bitter with the development of the second. The French Revolution attempted to resolve the situation by violence, but it only succeeded in abolishing the old regime and failed to construct anything new. In the event, therefore, there was a return to the institutions that had been destroyed. Having thus returned to the starting point, the regime which followed the Revolution continued to be based on social antagonisms, on the exploitation of man by man. The Saint-Simonians restated the conclusion of the master in a diptych which clearly pre-figures Marx's project: "The exploitation of man by man was the state of human relations in the past. The exploitation of nature by man cooperating with his fellow man is the picture which the future presents."

But Marx, while laying under contribution the ideas common to the Saint-Simonians and the Socialists who had preceded him, gave to the conflict of the social classes (a conflict different from the one which Saint-Simon had in mind) a radically different meaning. His explanation of past history at the beginning of the *Communist Manifesto* may be allowed to pass since its simplifications are tolerable in a pamphlet, but they are inadmissible in a historical work based on a scientific foundation. The class struggle changes its character when Marx connects it with Hegel's parable of the development of consciousness in the *Phenomenology of Mind* —the dialectic of Master and Slave or, perhaps more correctly, the dialectic of the *Bildung* (culture). This dialectical parable of consciousness is then transferred to economic and social life, but Marx never examines the conditions under which such an operation is possible. It is taken for granted in Marx's project as sketched by Engels as early as in 1844, and which consists in interpreting the categories of the "classical" political economy in terms of those of Hegelian philosophy. There is no denying that this is the case both in the *Economic and Philosophical Manuscripts of 1844* and in the *Heilige Familie* where certain pages, by the Hegelian vocabulary in which they are written and in the development of the ideas, make the transposition obvious. The necessary character of the situation in the Hegelian parable recurs in Marx's conception of the class struggle, so that the logical development of this situation leads to the positing of this conception as a law of historical development. Doubtless Marx does not state this in so many words, but his successors do not fail to do so. This law appeals to the mind and the imagination with far more force than the dialectical law of contradiction between the conditions of existence and the awareness of these conditions which man acquires, or the law of contradiction between production relationships and production forces.

It is of course a fact that the historian discovers certain types of class struggle, and a clash of interests in both the economic and the social fields, between men living in society. But to believe that the class struggle is the motive force of history is quite another matter and assumes that all the other conflicts which arise among men are reducible to clashes of interest in the economic field. No sociologist would admit that such a reduction is possible.

Marxism is also a philosophy of history since it introduces the concept of an "economic and social formation". Marx does this in the preface to *A Critique of Political Economy*. The "forms of production" are then moments in a single totality, stages in the evolution of this totality.

But this is only possible because Karl Marx *reduces* all social relationships to production relationships, "material social relationships", as Lenin wrote. This makes it possible to affirm and verify a regularly recurring pattern in the various economic systems. Lenin pays homage to Marx for this reduction which in his view makes "a scientific sociology" possible.

By the same token, this is to exclude from an analysis of economic systems all that gives each of them its special and distinctive character—institutions, mechanisms, the motives called into play for the furtherance of the common aim, the ideas which govern societies, etc. More accurately, it is to transfer these to the superstructure, that sphere where the human mind produces its products under conditions of exploitation, and such products therefore proceed from a warped human consciousness.

Doubtless, it could be pointed out that the assertion of the primacy of material conditioning in such a philosophy of history appears as an act of revenge taken by what *exists* against what is abstract, by man-in-the-concrete-situation against ideal awareness, by the existential against the ideal. All this is certainly present in Marx's philosophy. But this assertion is set in an analysis of human society achieved by the aid of concepts that have not been submitted to adequate criticism and are linked to the Marxist concept of man as wholly defined by his material needs.

For all practical purposes "social" for Marx equals "economic". His writings as a whole bear this out. It is obvious, for instance, if one reads the chapter on cooperation in *Capital* or Engels's *Anti-Dühring*. In *Wages, Prices and Profit*, Marx indeed observed that "social" has a wider meaning than "economic". He then wrote "this adjective 'social' has many implications". But this remark cannot do duty for the analysis which Marx barely outlined and never continued.

This original deficiency in Marx's analysis has, among others, two important consequences. It leads him to exclude Politics from the sphere of social relationships, to dismiss the State as belonging to society's superstructures. In the long run, Politics will have its revenge for this exclusion. The State will become the principal element, the creator and controller of these relationships. Economics and Politics having been placed at different levels of social life, the one in dependence upon the other (in theory at least), will no longer maintain a genuine dialectical relationship with one another, even though it has to be admitted that they exercise a certain mutual reciprocal influence.

This defective analysis also leads Marx to exclude from "social relationships", as he sees them, Law, Morality and Religion, and to consider them as elements in the super-structure and as conditioned by Economics. Here again, reality will give the lie to these ideas, especially if and when circumstances make it necessary to include under the same formulas a reality quite distinct from that which they are intended to convey.

Secondly, it leads Marx to consider these manifestations of human activity as mystifications and to classify them under the pejorative heading of "ideology". Lenin himself gives the lie to this conception when he attaches a value to the concept of ideology and in practice identifies it with Marxism itself in his expression "revolutionary ideology".

The identification of "social" with "economic" allows Marx

to treat all human knowledge and values as relative by making them dependent upon the development of the productive forces of society, by seeing in them the by-product of man's economic behaviour considered as fundamental. This devaluation of the spheres of human thought which "have no history and no development", since they have lost "all appearance of autonomy", was possible for Marx because of his affinity with Hegel from whom he had borrowed the notion of historical totality. Hegel's introduction of the theme of "the trick of the Idea" according to which Man's subjective beliefs are merely the jumping-off ground for the real development of the concept, prepares the way for Marx. Human thought becomes a historical phenomenon depending on a fundamental reality. For Hegel this reality is the Idea.

For Marx this reality is economic. For both men, the category of totality thus plays an essential rôle. "The convictions of existing persons do not depend on the social existence of these persons in any partial sense. It is the totality of their mental world, the total superstructure which is dependent upon their social existence."

Finally, it leads Marx to posit only one single bond between social reality and intellectual phenomena. For him, every intellectual attitude is dictated by an underlying material interest. In his *Introduction to the Critique of Hegel's Philosophy of Right* (1843), he assigned to German philosophical criticism the task of denouncing the social state of Germany. It is then easy for him to go on to unmask the ideologies. He therefore sees the *raison d'être* of the latter in vested interests alone.

The motivation of ideologies by interests is one of several forms by means of which the adoption of certain attitudes may be conditioned by a social experience. But it is not the only form which can exist between a social group and its intellectual positions. It is undoubtedly true that certain of these positions are adopted because they favour the interests of a group. A given economic theory, given political ideas, may be upheld by a group of men because they square with their interests. But this is no longer the case in other spheres of human activity, that of the arts for instance, even though the adoption of this or that style may be the result of a given historical and social conditioning. Every economic system is, in actual fact, included in a given intellectual universe. This is as true of the Soviet socialist system as it is of the capitalist system. On this particular point, the fact that Lenin places a value on the concept of ideology by making Marx-Leninism the ideology of the revolutionary class, partly gives the lie to Marx's ideas.

The deficiencies of Marx's analysis of the term "social", linked as they are with variations in the meaning he gives to the word "nature" (and we shall not examine these here) as well as his definition of Communism ("humanism in so far as it is integral naturalism, naturalism in so far as it is integral humanism"), lead to that idea of man which dominates the whole history of Marx-Leninism, and which Communism proposes to make a concrete reality, namely that of "total man". A Marxist philosopher has said of this "total man" that "he is the subject of action and at the same time the final object of action, its product even when it seems to be producing objects external to him. Total man is the living subject, at first torn asunder, disintegrated and chained to necessity and abstraction. He passes through this state of disintegration on his way towards freedom, he becomes nature, but a free nature. He becomes a totality like nature, but by dominating nature." This is not the place to discuss the whole complex of theses underlying these assertions. We nevertheless note with J. Hyppolite that the Marxist production of man seeks to be, "in spite of certain over-objective expressions of Marx, that Absolute which is a subject, man universal, the God who creates himself in the place of the God contemplated in a far-off heaven; 'man appropriates to himself his universal being in a universal way, in so far therefore as he is total man' (Karl Marx)". This total man, this "supreme example" of Communist humanism, rejects all reference to any kind of Absolute, especially to any kind of personal Absolute.

We come finally to the fact that Communist man becomes that "most valuable form of capital" of which Stalin spoke. He is dominated by economics and by his fellow men since nobody, not even Lenin, can guarantee that a Communist society will one day be achieved, and because, as Albert Camus remarks, the best way to promote community life under these conditions is by a reign of terror.

Although Marxism is engaged in the praiseworthy and desirable enterprise of delivering man from exploitation, of helping him to find freedom by creating it in spite of the resistance of things and of men, yet Marxist history finally leads not to a respect for the human person but to contempt for it. For man ultimately submits to the historical process as though it were his inescapable fate, whereas it should be for him the locus of a personal option which involves the whole of his destiny.

The interest shown in history by the Marxist seems to the Christian a transference on to the secular plane of the religious *meaning and direction* which he himself sees in the evolution of humanity. It is Christianity which introduced the fact and the idea of development, from the moment when man's salvation became operative in time, from the moment when the coming into the world of Christ, the incarnate Word of God, marked off past from future, since it introduced into human time an asymmetry which orientates it towards its goal. It is in the death and resurrection of Christ that the whole of human history finds its freedom, its progress and its salvation. It is because Christ has risen, it is because he gathers to himself the whole universe of man, that the Christian finds a meaning in his own life and his own death, and in the work which he does in this world. In a word, he finds that he is delivered from the final and ultimate exploitation of the man for whom history either has no goal or none other than nature.

THE CHRISTIAN COUNTER-POSITION

Communism, as we have said, is a philosophy of history and a practical philosophy, a *praxis* which proposes to bring into being that atheist, Godless universe in which man would appropriate to himself the creative power formerly attributed to God.

In this respect, Communism differs from all previous or present forms of rationalist atheism, which are satisfied with a philosophical denial that has no practical result, and abandon humanity to its state of exploitation.

Although it is essential to bring to light the radical antitheses existing between Communism and Christianity as well as the elements in Marx-Leninism open to scientific criticism, yet the Christian cannot remain satisfied with this absolutely necessary task, and for two reasons. Firstly, because he would be led to treat Marx-Leninism as an ordinary philosophical system, one among other conceptions of the world, that has only to be criticized, while he forgets that it is a form of action, a *praxis*, that has every intention of transforming the world which, in its view, all philosophy previous to itself has been content merely to contemplate. Secondly, because every Catholic is in duty bound to work for the advent of a human world increasingly quickened by the spirit of the Gospel, the spirit of justice and love, a world in which every man's life is itself so conditioned that it may be worthy of that image of God which he is. To refuse this obligation would be to fall into the error which, in another connection, Pius XII called "unilateral supernaturalism", under the pretext that we live in the world of the Redemption and are thereby withdrawn from the order of nature.[3]

Face to face with the Communist world the Christian, the

[3] Pius XII, *Christmas Message*, 1954.

Catholic, must act. But any sort of action will not do. Certain forms might lead to something much worse. What then is ours to be?

If the Christian wants to throw light on this difficult question, it would perhaps be as well for him to begin by asking himself why "the lure of Communism" has had its effect upon such great masses of men in our time, leaving aside for the moment the fact that Communist regimes have been established in the European People's Democracies and in China by means other than revolution or spontaneous and free consent.

Various inquiries made in France and Italy during the past ten years, the personal reflections of Communists, whether published or not, have revealed a great variety of reasons for the attraction that Communism has for our contemporaries. They vary from country to country, from one social group to another. We cannot catalogue them here, still less evaluate their relative importance.

However, the mass of information obtained seems to show that it is somewhat exceptional for adults to join the Communist movement after a careful, private study of the capitalist regime, uninfluenced either directly or indirectly by Marxism, as was the case with Jules Guesde for instance, after the war of 1870. He sided with Marx after fairly extensive private study. Yet we still occasionally find that a young man, born in a certain social milieu and with a taste for reading, will take the road that leads from the rationalism characteristic of the French school and of French science to Engels's *Anti-Dühring* and Lenin's *Left-Wing Communism and Infantile Diseases*. This road by-passes the "illusion of poetic enthusiasm", a conviction based on sentiment, which was frequent in France during the years 1944–6. Along such a path, Catholicism may well appear as a hypothesis which "has behind it a thousand years of failure", while the "Marx-Leninist dogmatic attitude is our loyalty to experience as established a century ago by Marx. And it is infinitely more cogent." Scientific progress too may well appear to fit normally into the Marxist hypothesis, even if it is not clear how scientific discoveries and progress can be included in a scientific system that owes its dynamic force to the dialectic and is accompanied by an anti-religious philosophical interpretation of a metaphysical character.

Although it has played an important part in the conversion of many Christians to Communism, we can only mention the conscious or unconscious confusion in their minds between the Kingdom of God and the advent of the classless society, between Christian and Marxist eschatology. This confusion has been made easy by the undoubted generosity of these Christians and still more by the ambiguous vocabulary used by Communism in its propaganda and public utterances— justice, the significance of human life, liberty, and many other concepts have, in the Communist vocabulary, neither the sense nor the characteristics attributed to them by the Christian.

The "troubled conscience" of the intellectual who feels he is useless or lost in a universe where work, profit, efficiency become the key-values, and a certain form of pragmatism which seeks to justify itself by philosophical arguments, also play their part and have succeeded in effecting a conversion which refuses to keep open certain questions, by simply ruling them out of order.

But the motive which in the majority of cases leads to mass conversions is the refusal to tolerate the unjust conditions of the vast majority of men in the industrial society which followed the agrarian societies of previous centuries.

It is poverty above all which gives it members and troops, a poverty which there is scarcely any need to describe, it is so glaringly obvious. Even so, there is less of it in France than in many other countries, where 1,500 million men are still underfed. Although it is less prevalent than a century ago, it continues to be widespread. The proletariat is not a meaningless word but a terrible reality which degrades and dehumanizes a large part of the human race, making man a kind of pariah "camping", as Auguste Comte put it, rather than established in society. Paltry wages, inadequate housing, which makes a moral life extremely difficult, deplorable working conditions in industry, lack of intellectual culture, practical slavery of mind and body, anxiety as to what the morrow may bring, future insecurity in face of the continuous threat of unemployment or crises, difficulties in family life and the education of the children. . . . All this is the result of an immense *injustice*, of a monstrous inequality in the distribution of material and spiritual goods, an injustice whose cause must be sought in the egoism, avarice, will to power and pride of those in possession, but also in social structures and the institutions in which this egoism is incarnate.[4]

Any man who has lived this life to the depths in his own flesh and blood, will be tempted to see only in Communism "the movement which will effectively do away with the present situation" according to one of Karl Marx's definitions. Communism will then appear as the consciousness of the proletariat, its "inherent philosophy".

These few indications are not an essay in the typology of conversions to Communism, but they are sufficient for our purpose, incomplete though they are, since they show that the Catholic must bring his thought and action to bear in a twofold direction as he faces Communism. There must be:

1. A process of religious reflection which will reveal the fact that Christianity by consecrating the universe as a whole to God, makes it ready to receive its one unique vocation.

2. A course of action whose mainspring is essentially a witness to the love of Christ on both the personal and the institutional planes.

In a world which is changing with a rapidity of which we

[4] E. Rideau, *Le Communisme, ses causes, sa forme actuelle, sa séduction*, Lecture given to the Institut Catholique of Paris, December 1950, p. 4.

are all aware—to stress it is a commonplace—one task awaits
the Christian which the fact of Communism makes only more
urgent, namely, that of a twofold movement in depth—a
deepening of religion brought about by a study of the Tradi-
tion of the Church increasingly known and loved, a deeper
critical appreciation of the progress of the sciences, which will
liberate them from all the metaphysical opinions unconsciously associated with them, in order that the core of their
reality may be grasped. To be more precise, we need a twofold
process of reflection—an upward movement of thought towards the universe as known to the sciences, a downward
movement towards this universe itself from the point of view
of God and of the spiritual values. This twofold movement in
depth will make it possible for Christianity to achieve that
consecration of the world which is symbolized in the great
cathedrals of the Middle Ages in sculpture and stained glass
—those fearless witnesses to thought and to faith. (I am thinking in particular of the arching in the doorway of the kings
at Chartres.)

Doubtless "the problem of progress is a thorny one, since
the general bent of men's characters and their individual
prejudices give different directions to dogmatic debate".[5]
Doubtless the demands of the task which we have outlined
are immense—we need, among other things, exceptional scientific knowledge and humility, both intellectual and spiritual.
Doubtless, too, we must tread a narrow path if we are to avoid
the stumbling-blocks of fideism, modernism and the doctrine
of inevitable progress. Yet surely it is not impossible in our
times, when science is ever enlarging the sphere of human
activity, to attempt to think out and do what the sculptors of
the cathedrals represented in symbolic form at the time when,
with Aristotle's help, the sciences began to enter the Christian
world.

[5] E. Rideau, *Consécration, le christianisme et l'activité humaine*,
Desclée de Brouwer, Paris, 1945, p. 72.

It is upon this task undertaken in a spirit of faith and loyalty to the Church, that we largely depend if Communists are to be able one day to recognize Christ as God and Saviour of all men. "The only key to the difficulties arising between the apparent materialism of science and the faith is to be found in a healthy understanding of the relations between mind and matter, soul and body, God and the world."[6] This is equally true in part of Marxist materialism.

If Communism were only a materialist concept of the world, emphasizing the forces that condition human life, this is as far perhaps as the Christian might go. But the Marxism which inspires Communism is a doctrine of action, and Communism is a movement.

This movement intends to establish an atheist order of society where every religious or metaphysical problem will be banished from man's consciousness by the existence of economic and social structures which will ensure the complete and absolute freedom of man, by a critique of the behaviour of the religious man that finally reduces religion to the status of a mere ideological illusion; and by a critique of the daily life of institutions existing under the previous regime, the Church in particular.

The Christian is thus enlisted in a course of action which moves at levels that are recognizably different but yet must remain a unity. In the first place, a Christian attitude and action are a duty in conscience for every Catholic on the personal and institutional planes, in the spheres of economic, social and political life with their ascending scale of values. For, although this present world is not the goal towards which the Christian moves, it is the "way to our true home (*patria*)", as St Augustine reminded Christians dismayed by the barbarian invasion of Italy. It must already foreshadow, through the relations it establishes among men, the "mansions" pre-

[6] P. Chauchard, *La science détruit-elle la religion?* Paris, 1958, p. 37.

pared by our heavenly Father. The Christian cannot hold aloof from the great tasks incumbent upon mankind—to feed and care for men, to free slaves—because he is a Christian, but also because he is a man living in a given society, a given universe, among particular men with particular problems to solve—housing, wages, education, work problems, etc. "The most harmonious human societies", wrote Fr Teilhard de Chardin in *Études* (1939), "seem to us to be in the last analysis the products not of segregation but of synthesis."

Among the popes, Pius XI and Pius XII in particular, as well as the bishops, have reminded us, and continue insistently to remind us, of the urgency of this Christian action, concerned as it is with both persons and institutions. It ought not therefore to be necessary to insist upon it again here, were one not forced to note that Catholics as a body—with the exception of an *élite*—have too often taken no notice of this teaching or have only responded to this appeal by limiting it to personal or family problems. There are many Catholics who neglect the problems raised by social, economic and political life, or who approach them either with the prejudices of the last century or with the intention of acting without reference to man's relationships with God. They thus lead a partly double life, disastrous to faith in each case.

In this course of action which—under certain conditions clearly laid down by the Church—brings the Catholic into contact with the Communist, he must beware of any practical attitude that would end by making him an atheist or materialist on the plane of reason and his daily life in human society, while he remains a true believer on the plane of faith.

Not that we have to refuse to work for a true humanism if we are really to find God, not that we have to refuse to christianize the human values on which Communism in its own way has again insisted—work, society, a thirst for justice—but this work of christianization demands that we refuse to live this

partly double life which would make it possible for us to
lead our human existence as atheists, while recovering our
Christianity on another plane, whose relevance to man as he
really is, we are unable to determine.[7]

The same may be said, and with equal force, of the Christian who is daily at grips with a world of techniques, and
technical, economic and financial institutions, which disregard
in practice the Christian ends of man. If we wish to control
things alone, we end up by treating men as things, as objects.
This is a more subtle danger and no less a one for being less
obvious and less insisted upon.

But atheistic Communism's challenge to Christianity demands of the Christian that this action should move on a
higher plane, for Marxist atheism is at one and the same time
a challenge to *religion* and to *faith*.

The Marxist temptation at the sociological level involves
the whole mystery of the relations of God and man which
Scripture calls *religion* (James 1. 27), *piety* (1 Timothy 3. 16),
faith and *Gospel* in St Paul and St Mark, and whose meaning
is summed up in Col. 1. 27: "Christ in us, the hope of glory."
This *faith* in Christ is *religion* par excellence. It is not *of* this
world although it is *in* it, and it cannot be reduced to a figure
of this world which passes away. But it demands that, as we
face every issue, we should first of all be aware of its divine
origin.[8]

In this our world where the Church of Christ is the sign
and sacrament of his presence among us, a right attitude to
the Church is required at the outset. This attitude may be
distorted in two ways. "The faults of her members may cause
us to lose sight of the inviolable mystery of the Church or we
may use this mystery as an alibi for our sins as Christians."[9]

[7] G. Martelet, "L'athéisme marxiste, tentation et réveil du chrétien",
Revue de L'Action Populaire, No. 111, 1957, p. 907.
[8] G. Martelet, *op. cit.*, p. 906.
[9] G. Martelet, *op. cit.*, p. 910.

In the first case we forget the holiness of the Church which transcends the sinfulness of each and all of her members. In the second case we forget that this holiness of the Church is not *ipso facto* our own. Both attitudes are denials in practice of the true dimensions of the mystery of the Church and give occasion for the attacks of atheistic Communism.

During the Communist persecution in Czecho-Slovakia, one of the People's Democracies, a group of priests in a concentration camp recorded their reflections on their past life and came to the following conclusions:

> We have too often forgotten that Christ came to serve and not to be served. We have taken advantage of our spiritual dignity in order to take our place in the ranks of those who are served. Our material conditions of life have perhaps not been modelled on those of evangelical poverty. We have often had more than enough to eat. We have lived in well-warmed houses and had no thought for Christ suffering hunger and shivering with the cold in his brethren at our very doors. . . . Should not our houses have been living centres of the love of Christ? "Show us the love which you have preached and of which you have written", said the Communists to us.
>
> In the social conflicts of our times, we have often—to all intents and purposes—lent our support to the wealthy. At least, we have not dared to protest against social injustices for fear of losing the alms of our benefactors who, in any case, were not always the most fervent of Christians. All this has given the poor and the workers the impression that we do not belong to their own but to the ruling class. In places where there were priests who not only spoke of love but practised it, places where priests lived who engaged in an intensive social apostolate, Communism finds it difficult to gain a foothold and the Communist's accusations against priests as enemies of the people carry no weight. This lesson may seem severe. Indeed it is. But in criticizing our past religious life severely, we have no intention of decrying it. The religious life of our country was intense and vital. It still is . . . But after we were deported,

what we most regretted . . . was that we had given our flocks insufficient preparation for an epoch which calls for *heroism* and *genuine* saints.[10]

This is an important testimony for it occurs in the context of a balanced and subtle analysis of the situation of Catholics in a People's Democracy. It is a testimony which we cannot ignore. It invites all Christians, both priests and laymen, to an effort of purification.

Another testimony, this time China, makes it equally clear that atheistic Communism has been kept in check by a complete and unconditional loyalty to the mystery of the Church in all its dimensions, regardless of the imperfections of her members.

Nearer home, thirty years spent at Ivry, in contact with a living, active Communism, have led to the same conclusion:

It seems that Marxism whose promises have destroyed all true hope, requires the presence of apostolic men whose religion is pure and undefiled and who freely give their lives to the demands of God's love. I would write the word *Church* on every line as often as I wrote the word *God*. Marxist atheism despises God and the Church but love *will not tolerate*, cannot bear with, contempt for what it loves.[11]

What therefore is demanded of the Christian, in the face of Marxist atheism, is both a witness and an apostolate of love. Let us listen once more to the priests from behind the Iron Curtain:

When the Church in our country was deprived of all the modern methods of the apostolate, . . we saw that in addition to prayer there is another way of engaging in the apostolate which nobody can take from us. . . . This apostolate of practical, heartfelt, effective love is absolutely essential. It is the

[10] A. Michel, *Problèmes religieux dans un pays sous régime communiste*, Ed. Fleurus, Paris, 1955, pp. 59–60.

[11] M. Delbrel, *Ville marxiste, terre de mission*, Ed. du Cerf, Paris, 1957, p. 12.

most eloquent, the most powerful, the most persuasive Christian apologetic.[12]

This is a testimony and an apostolate of loyalty to the mystery of the Church. They accept the mystery of her holiness (difficult to grasp though it may be). For it is because she is faithful to her mission to preach Christ, and not on account of her own weaknesses, that the Church is attacked by Communism—whether directly or indirectly is of little consequence in this connection. It is because she is faithful to her mission to proclaim to mankind, in the name of God himself, the true nature of man, that Communism, which proposes to create a Godless mankind, takes up its stand against the Church. But as long as it continues tirelessly to maintain its claim to produce a Godless mankind, and for this reason alone, Communism will find in the Church its living, spiritual opponent.

[12] A. Michel, *op. cit.*, p. 81.

SELECT BIBLIOGRAPHY

BERDYAEV, N.: *Origin of Russian Communism*, London, Bles, 1937, and Naperville, Ill., Allenson; *The Russian Revolution*, London and New York, Sheed and Ward, 1931.

D'ARCY, Martin, S.J.: *Communism and Christianity*, London and Baltimore, Penguin, 1956.

DAWSON, Christopher: *Religion and the Modern State*, London and New York, Sheed and Ward, 1938.

FANFANI, Amintore: *Catholicism, Protestantism and Capitalism*, London and New York, Sheed and Ward, 1935.

FREMANTLE, Anne: (Editor) *The Papal Encyclicals in Their Historical Context*, New York, New American Library of World Literature, 1956. See also: *Selected Papal Encyclicals and Letters*, London, Catholic Truth Society, 1939—

GURIAN, Waldemar: *Bolshevism*, translated from the German by E. I. Watkin, London and New York, Sheed and Ward, 1932.

GURIAN, W. and FITZSIMMONS, M. A.: *The Catholic Church in World Affairs*, Oxford, Blackwell, and Indiana, Notre Dame, Ind., Notre Dame Univ. Press, 1954.

HYDE, Douglas: *Answer to Communism*, London, Paternoster Publications, 1951; *I Believed*, London, Pan Books, 1956; *The Mind Behind New China*, London, Paternoster Publications, 1956.

MARITAIN, Jacques, *Man and the State* (edited by O'Sullivan, B.), London, Hollis and Carter, 1954, and Chicago, Univ. of Chicago Press, 1955; *The Twilight of Civilization*, translated from the French by L. Landry, London and New York, Sheed and Ward, 1946.

MENCZER, B. (Editor): *Catholic Political Thought, 1789–1848*, Oxford, Blackwell, and Notre Dame, Ind., Notre Dame Univ. Press, 1952.

RYAN, J. A. and BOLAND, F. F.: *Catholic Principles of Politics*, New York, Macmillan, 1940.

SHEED, F. J., *Communism and Man*, London and New York, Sheed and Ward, 1945.

SHEEN, Fulton J.: *Communism and the Conscience of the West*, Dublin, Browne and Nolan, and Indianapolis, Bobbs, 1948.

WATT, L.: *Communism and Religion*, London, Catholic Truth Society.

The Twentieth Century Encyclopedia
of Catholicism

*The number of each volume indicates its place in
the over-all series and not the order of publication.*

TWENTIETH CENTURY ENCYCLOPEDIA OF CATHOLICISM

All titles are subject to change.